STUDY SKILLS FOR PROFESSIONAL STUDENTS IN HIGHER EDUCATION

Dr. M. ADITHAN
Profesor Emeritus
VIT University, Vellore (Tamil Nadu)

S. CHAND
PUBLISHING

S Chand And Company Limited
(ISO 9001 Certified Company)

S.CHAND
PUBLISHING

S Chand And Company Limited

(ISO 9001 Certified Company)

Head Office: Block B-1, House No. D-1, Ground Floor, Mohan Co-operative Industrial Estate, New Delhi – 110 044 | Phone: 011-66672000

Registered Office: A-27, 2nd Floor, Mohan Co-operative Industrial Estate, New Delhi – 110 044
Phone: 011-49731800

www.**schandpublishing.com**; e-mail: **info@schandpublishing.com**

Branches

Chennai	:	Ph: 23632120; chennai@schandpublishing.com
Guwahati	:	Ph: 2738811, 2735640; guwahati@schandpublishing.com
Hyderabad	:	Ph: 40186018; hyderabad@schandpublishing.com
Jalandhar	:	Ph: 4645630; jalandhar@schandpublishing.com
Kolkata	:	Ph: 23357458, 23353914; kolkata@schandpublishing.com
Lucknow	:	Ph: 4003633; lucknow@schandpublishing.com
Mumbai	:	Ph: 25000297; mumbai@schandpublishing.com
Patna	:	Ph: 2260011; patna@schandpublishing.com

First Edition 2014

ISBN: 978-93-837-4644-6 **Product Code:** H3SOS64VOCA20ENAA14O

PRINTED IN INDIA

By Vikas Publishing House Private Limited, Plot 20/4, Site-IV, Industrial Area Sahibabad, Ghaziabad – 201 010 and Published by S Chand And Company Limited, A-27, 2nd Floor, Mohan Co-operative Industrial Estate, New Delhi – 110 044.

PREFACE

Engineering Colleges and Technical Institutions in India are an important segment in the Indian Higher Education System. They have made tremendous impact on and contribution to the Indian economy. India is making giant strides, through its expanding and invigorating educational system, to assume a significant role in the International scenario.

To promote continuing engineering education, research and innovation in their professional life, engineers and technologists need to be trained while they are pursuing their Engineering and Technology Degree Programmes in Engineering Colleges and Technical Institutions itself. This book will give the desired study skills, inputs and exposure to them right in the early stages of their education and training, in that they become adequately and well-trained engineering professionals ready to enter and serve the world of work.

Studying in a College or University provides an opportunity for students to transition into adulthood through a continuous development of one's beliefs, desires, aspirations, goals, values, personality and changing life-styles.

Engineering College students require training in a number of skills to complement their knowledge gained in the chosen professional field of engineering.

Life and study in an engineering college should be fully engaging, fruitful, enjoyable, memorable, professionally enriching and rewarding and should prepare the students with necessary competencies, not only for the immediate job or career opportunities but also to equip them to meet the economic, social and technological challenges of the future.

This compendium (book) is a step in this direction. It is sincerely hoped that the Engineering Professionals will be highly benefitted by this book.

Dr. M. ADITHAN

This Page has been intentionally left blank

ACKNOWLEDGEMENT

I would like to acknowledge and thank Dr. Raymond B. Landis, Dean Emeritus, College of Engineering and Technology, California State University, Los Angeles, USA for the slide presentations he has made available : "Studying Engineering : A Road Map to a Rewarding Career: 3rd ed., April 2007" for wider dissemination amongst engineering college students and faculty. Some portions of this text/book have been based on and adapted from the above-mentioned work/reference.

Dr. M. ADITHAN

This Page has been intentionally left blank

CONTENTS

This Page has been intentionally left blank

1
CHAPTER

WHAT IS ENGINEERING?

What is engineering? How would you respond?

"Engineering is the profession in which the knowledge of mathematical and natural sciences (physics and chemistry) gained by study, experience and practice, is applied with judgement to develop ways to utilize economically, the materials and the methods for the benefit of mankind"

GREATEST ENGINEERING ACHIEVEMENTS OF 20TH CENTURY

- High performance materials
- Nuclear technology
- Laser and fiber optics
- Petroleum and gas technology
- Health technology
- Household appliances
- Imaging technology
- Internet and E-Mail
- Space exploration
- Interstate highways
- Refrigeration and Air-conditioning
- Telephone, Mobile/Cellular phones
- Computers and Super computers
- Agricultural mechanization
- Radio and television
- Electronics
- Safe and affordable water
- Supersonic aircrafts
- Automobiles
- Power plants and Electrification

REWARDS AND OPPORTUNITIES OF AN ENGINEERING CAREER

- Job satisfaction
- Variety of job opportunities and career options

- Challenging work
- Intellectual development
- Social impact
- Financial security and good salary
- Prestige
- Professional environment
- Understanding how things work and product development
- Creative thinking
- Critical thinking

Major Engineering and Technology Disciplines

- Civil Engineering
- Mechanical Engineering
- Electrical Engineering
- Electronics Engineering
- Computer Engineering
- Chemical Engineering
- Industrial Engineering
- Aerospace Engineering/Aeronautical Engineering
- Bio-Technology
- Biomedical Engineering
- Information Technology
- Agricultural Engineering
- Automobile Engineering/Automotive Technology
- Communication Engineering/Telecommunication Engineering
- Petroleum Engineering
- Systems Engineering
- Nuclear Engineering
- Space Science and Technology
- Mining Engineering
- Armament Technology

Criteria for Engineering Education (A-K)

a. An ability to apply knowledge of mathematics, science and engineering.

b. An ability to design and conduct experiments as well as to analyze and interpret data.

c. An ability to design a system, component or process to meet the desired needs.

d. An ability to function on multi-disciplinary teams.

e. An ability to identify, formulate and solve engineering problems.

f. An understanding of professional and ethical responsibility.

g. An ability to communicate effectively.

h. A broad education necessary to understand the impact of engineering solutions in a global and societal context.

i. A recognition of the need for and an ability to engage in life-long learning.

j. A knowledge of contemporary issues.

k. An ability to use techniques, skills and modern engineering tools necessary for engineering practice.

Engineering Job Functions

- Analysis, Simulation and Modeling
- Design
- Prototype development
- Testing
- Construction and Development
- Procurement and System Integration
- Sales, Marketing and Advertising
- Research and Development
- Business and Management
- Consulting/ Consultancy Services
- Teaching/Technical Training
- Entrepreneurship

Functions of Engineering Professionals

Within a given engineering field of specialization there are many functional areas in which engineers are engaged. These are:

- **Research and Development:** seeking new knowledge and for better understanding, for development of new equipment, products, processes, technology and methods
- **Design:** converting the concept into detailed plan and drawing of specifications of equipment, machines and materials
- **Production/Manufacturing:** involving machines, equipment and processes by which products/ components are made from raw materials
- **Construction:** the process of converting design into structures, buildings, bridges, highways, machine building, power plants, transmission lines and communication facilities, erection using appropriate equipment, materials and processes

- **Operations:** the application of engineering and management principles in carrying out manufacturing, inspection, procuring of engineering items, assembly, performance testing directing and controlling of operating personnel, servicing and maintenance
- **Sales and Marketing:** understanding customers' needs, supplying appropriate equipment/ product and spares, providing after sales service and maintenance
- **Management:** involving policy planning, corporate affairs, finance, organizational structure, public relations, recruitment, selection and training of engineers and managers and coordination of R&D, production, sales and marketing and ensuring profitability

Employment Opportunities

- Professional, scientific and technical services
- Design, research and development
- Information services
- Construction
- Retailing, sales and marketing
- Administrative and support services
- Management of companies
- Small business development
- Testing, Quality and Certification
- Software development
- Mining
- Repair maintenance and re-conditioning services
- Welding and Fabrication

Various Job Titles Assigned to Engineering Graduates

1. Engineer/Assistant Engineer/Executive Engineer/Assistant Executive Engineer
2. Superintending Engineer/Chief Engineer
3. Senior Engineer
4. Field Engineer
5. Test Engineer
6. Sales Engineer
7. Design Engineer
8. Research Engineer
9. Flight Engineer
10. Manager (Engineering)
11. Quality Control Engineer
12. Civil Engineer/Mechanical Engineer/Electrical Engineer/Electronics Engineer/Instruments Engineer /Tele-Communication Engineer/Mining Engineer/Computer Engineer/Armament

Engineer/Aeronautical Engineer/Foundry Engineer/Welding Engineer/ Petroleum Engineer (depending on the professional area in which the engineer is employed)

13. Maintenance Engineer
14. Site/Construction Engineer
15. Tool Engineer/Methods Engineer
16. Manufacturing Engineer/Production Engineer/Quality Control Engineer/Industrial Engineer
17. Systems Engineer
18. Bio-Medical Engineer
19. Manager/Works Manager
20. Works Supdt.
21. Metallurgist Engineer
22. Foreman/Senior Foreman
23. Oil Rigs Engineer
24. Garrison Engineer/Military Engineer

The Engineer's Role

More than a discipline or a body of knowledge, engineering is a verb, an action verb, denoting a way of approaching a problem.

— ***Scott Whitmire***

Basic principle of engineering education is **"problem solving"**. Problem solving is an acquired skill, and one that no engineer can be without whether he is involved in creative design or in the analysis of existing systems, or products.

One of the key skills of an engineer is the **ability to "analyze"**. This ability will be only one fact of your professional personality as an engineer. You must also be **able to "synthesize"**, and, perhaps even more important, you must always seek and explore new ideas.

Many problem solving techniques have been developed, which you will study while pursuing a Degree Programme in the engineering college.

You will be taught by your professors how to bridge the gap between knowing a set of principles, applying these principles and solving the problems of engineering. Courses on Engineering Analysis are designed to impart these problems solving skills to engineering students.

Physics, Chemistry and Mathematics courses will help you to sharpen your mind and learn all the basic principles of the physical sciences. Hence they are important.

The real meaning and applicability of the principles must come from the student's own discovery as he attempts to solve the problems.

Basically, the engineer is a problem-solver. He must either provide a better solution to the problem than that which prevails now or develop a new solution which never existed.

The engineer's role is to bridge the gap between an idea and its physical reality by solving problems that exit between two extremes, very often with little to guide them except his intuition. This is called the "creativity gap".

The tools of the engineer are the scientific principles that have been formulated about the behaviour of the universe and its contents. The laws of motion, mechanisms, materials properties, matter, principles of thermodynamics, electricity and energy are some of the tools that permit the engineer to develop a workable solution to a problem.

The engineer must develop sufficient depth of understanding of the basic principles so that they become like tools for him. He must be able to devote his energy and effort to building a solution to a problem. An engineer has to immerse himself in the tasks/challenges of problem solving.

Very often in real-life problems which the engineers must solve, the application of principles may be the simplest part of the task. However, the challenging aspect is often the specific definition of a situation from which realistic answer or solution can be obtained for a vaguely stated problem. **In many real life situations, problems are not that much well defined. Understanding the complexities of the real problem and formulating the problem is itself a challenging job for the engineers, present and the future.**

Engineering students must be made aware of this while they are taught problem solving skills in the classrooms.

The Design Process

Generally in component or product design, three stages are involved:

1. Conceptual Design
2. Preliminary Design and
3. Detailed Design

During the **Conceptual Design** stage, geometry and materials are unknown, (*i.e.,* not yet identified). Techniques such as feature-based or solid modelling are used by the designer at this stage.

In the **Preliminary Design** stage, all of the materials and dimensions of the components/ product(s) are known.

In the final **Detailed Design** stage, all of the information about the components/product and how it is to be manufactured are known. This includes complete design details including dimensions, tolerances and finishes; the product support requirements and even the product disposal requirements; production/ manufacturing details, such as materials and processes standards, scheduling, economical lot sizes (batch sizes), processes and component/products functional requirements, testing, packaging and delivery of assembled/finished product.

The Engineering Design Process

The steps involved are:

- Identify the needs or requirements of the customer
- State the problem definition and the specifications of the equipment, machine or system
- Collect the relevant data and information
- Develop various alternative designs
- Evaluate various alternative solutions

- Select the optimal design or the design that meets your requirements
- Implement the optimal design

SIX SIGMA

Six Sigma is a quality control tool. Six Sigma is the most widely used strategy for statistical quality assurance (SQA) in industries today. This concept was originally popularized by Motorola in the 1980's. The Six Sigma strategy is a vigorous and disciplined methodology that uses data and statistical analysis to measure and improve an industry's operational performance by identifying and eliminating "defects" in manufacturing and service - related processes".

Six Sigma is derived from six standard deviations *i.e.* $\pm 3\sigma$ (equivalent to 3.4 defects per million occurrences) - indicates an extremely high quality standard. Higher the sigma level, the lower the defect rate and lower the defect rate, the higher the quality.

The Six Sigma methodology consists of the following 5 core steps:

1. **Define** customer requirements and deliverables through well defined methods of customer communication.
2. **Measure** the existing processes and their output to determine current quality performance by collecting defects metrics.
3. **Analyze** defect metrics (defect analysis) and determine the vital few causes.
4. **Improve** the processes by eliminating the root causes of defects.
5. **Control** the processes to ensure that future work doesn't reintroduce the causes of defects.

These steps are referred to DMAIC (Define, Measure, Analyse, Improve and Control) methodology.

Six Sigma strategy can be adopted in many areas of business/industry:

1. Product Design and Design Methodology
2. Continuous Process improvement
3. Continuous Product improvement
4. Enhanced Customer Satisfaction
5. Supply Chain Improvement/Supply Chain Management.

Six Sigma paves way for the enhancement of human elements such as Strong Leadership, Training and Development, Customer Focus, Project Teams and Culture Change.

CHAPTER 2

WHAT IS SUCCESS?

YOU CAN ACHIEVE SUCCESS!

- Academically poor students and average students have succeeded
- Highly qualified students have failed
- Then what makes the difference?

SUCCESS IS THE ACHIEVEMENT OF SOMETHING

- Desired
- Planned, or
- Attempted

FORMULA FOR SUCCESS

According to Shiv Khera, the famous and well known motivational speaker and author, your attitude, your values and your vision form the basis of your success. Anything is possible to achieve by motivating yourself with your positive thinking.

However, positive thinking alone, cannot guarantee success. Positive thinking, coupled with a well defined action plan, will yield success.

One's willpower more than skill contributes to one's success. Even though technical skill (hard skill) and people skill (soft skill) are essential, it is people skill that really matters and is of vital importance as you climb higher in your professional career.

By building cordial relationships many problems can be solved. If people skill is lacking, you cannot taste success.

Positive thinking and positive behaviour should become an integral part of one's life. Developing good habits are essential, for it greatly contributes to positive attitudes and positive thinking. Give importance to your reputation and most important to your character. Keep up your self-esteem.

Don't quit. Don't give up.

GOAL SETTING

How can you expect to get somewhere if you don't know where you want to go?

- Goal setting is important
- Goals give you something to measure yourself

- Goals give you direction for your life
- Hence you should know your goals and write down your goals as clearly as possible

How can you strengthen Your Commitment?

- By clarifying your goals, *i.e.,* explain your goals in clear terms
- Learn as much as you can about engineering and technology
- Prepare a road map which you can follow
- Work hard to achieve your goal

Ability Vs Effort

- Do you believe that people succeed because of their **ability** that some people "have it" while others don't?

(Or)

- Do you believe that people succeed because of their **effort**?

  Which do you think is more important?

  Ability or **Effort**? Why?

Fixed Mindset Vs Growth Mindset

People generally have one of these "Mindsets".

Fixed mindset: You believe that your talents and abilities are already set in you — either you have them or you don't have them.

(Or)

Growth Mindset: Talents can be developed and superior talents and greater abilities can be built over a period of time as one grows.

Both these mindsets are important and are required for success in engineering study.

CHAPTER 3

Success in Engineering Study Depends on

- Your Efforts - "Work Hard"
- Your Approach - "Work Smart", and
- Your Attitude - "Think Positively Always"

How should you view Your Education in the Engineering College?

- What knowledge, skills and attitudes will you acquire when you graduate?
- You should know what employers look for in new engineering graduates
- What can you do to ensure that you get a quality education during your engineering study?

When you Graduate from Engineering College you should Acquire

1. An ability to apply knowledge of mathematics, science and engineering
2. An ability to design and conduct experiments as well as to analyze and interpret data
3. An ability to design a system, component or process to meet desired needs *i.e.,* functional requirements
4. An ability to function in multi-disciplinary teams
5. An ability to identify, formulate and solve engineering problems
6. An ability to communicate effectively
7. An ability to use the techniques, skills and modern engineering tools (*e.g.* relevant Softwares) necessary for engineering practice
8. A broad education necessary to understand the impact of engineering solutions in a global and societal context.
9. An ability to **"learn how to learn"** *i.e.,* engage yourself in life-long learning
10. A knowledge of contemporary issues *i.e.,* issues concerning present generation.
11. An understanding of professional and ethical responsibility

What your Employers want when they Recruit you for Employment?

1. In addition to your qualifications, they look for maturity, initiative, enthusiasm, poise (balanced approach), good appearance, integrity, flexibility and ability to work with people (Team work).
2. Good grades in all subjects in your branch of engineering.

3. Whether you underwent any specialized course(s) relating to a particular field of work?
4. Ability to communicate effectively, both orally (Spoken English) and in writing (Written English)
5. Kind of industrial training or practical training you underwent while studying in engineering college
6. Experience in campus activities, especially participation and involvement in co-curricular activities (Seminars, Symposia, Workshops, Conferences and Professional Societies) and extra-curricular activities (Sports, Games, Cultural events, Students' Club activities)

Your Involvement as a Student in Campus Life

1. Your participation in various students organizations
2. Your interaction with faculty members
3. Your interaction with fellow students
4. How have you spent your time and energy in the campus apart from studying?

How was your Life Spent in Campus?

1. Stayed in hostel, or a day-scholar; arrangements you have made for living while studying?
2. Influence of family, parents and relatives?
3. Influence of class teachers/professors?
4. Influence of others, mentor, student adviser, project guide, proctor, warden?

Three Basic Skills

According to Tony Wagner, Harvard based education expert and author of "The Global Achievement Gap": Three basic skills that students should acquire if they want to thrive in a knowledge economy are:

1. The ability to do **critical thinking** and **problem solving**
2. The ability to **communicate effectively** and
3. The **ability to collaborate;**

Ten Life Skills which an Engineering Student should Acquire and Develop

- Empathy (putting oneself in another persons state of mind to understand his/her problems)
- Problem solving
- Inter-personal relationship
- Creative thinking
- Critical thinking
- Coping with stress
- Managing feeling of emotion
- Self-awareness
- Decision making
- Effective communication

4

CHAPTER

The Beginning of the Semester

Following are the activities that you should do at the beginning of each semester:

- Collect your course syllabus/ know the titles of the subjects you will be studying in this semester
- Note down the Time Table of your class/branch
- Acquire the relevant/ prescribed textbooks and other materials, design data book, if any, charts, problem sets or data sheets you may use in your tutorials, etc.

Preparing Yourself for Attending Lectures

- Review your class notes, read the chapters in the text, solve the problems, answer the questions listed at the end of the chapter(s).
- Sometimes lectures may be like a reinforcement to the subject matter you have already studied/learnt
- Everyday you should study a small portion of the subject matter and acquire the relevant knowledge (Do not postpone your studies to a latter day)

During the Class Periods

- As far as possible sit near the front; you will hear the teacher better and see the board clearly
- Concentrate on what the teacher is teaching/doing
- Develop good listening skills
- Take notes systematically
- If you have any doubt ask questions in the class and clarify your doubts

Characteristics of a Good Listener

What you should do:

- Consider that all topics are equally important
- Listen so that you acquire new knowledge/information
- Judge the value of the content rather than the style of the delivery of the teacher
- Listen and identify the central theme. This will help you to build anchor points to follow the entire lecture
- Be alert and listen carefully what the teacher says

- Note down the important points discussed in the class
- Avoid distractions and concentrate on what the Professor is saying
- Consider difficult portion discussed as an exercise for the mind
- Listen to the teacher with an open mind
- Think more deeply about what the lecturer is saying, try to summarize the topic that has been covered

How Should You Take Notes?

- Good notes help you to know what is important
- As far as possible, use spiral notebook in taking down notes in the class instead of a rigid/ bound register note book or stapled note book
- Listen to the teacher carefully and note down the important points or ideas discussed
- Draw the diagram, note down the equation or formula the teacher writes on the board

Professors and Teachers are important resources and they are costly resources which the Institute/College has acquired.

You Should Know

What Professors Do?

- To provide instructions to the students
- Academic advising, providing career guidance/counselling and personal advice to the students
- To monitor students' progress; and to involve them actively in the teaching-learning process
- To assess students' work/assignments/answer scripts/and award a Grade consistent with the students' academic performance
- To involve the students in research and development (R&D) activities to the extent possible depending on their abilities and interest
- To serve as a Reference/ Referee when students apply for a job or higher studies
- To recommend them for scholarships or for academic awards or for a job or for their higher studies

Characteristics of Your Professors

- Professors believe that their areas of subject matter specialty, their experience and their expertise are important to them.
- They are interested in advancing the knowledge in their areas of specialization by carrying out research and development (R&D) and publishing papers in international and national Journals and presenting papers in conferences/ symposia
- They have chosen an academic career over professional practice or working in a company/ organisation/industry
- They believe they are outstanding teachers and have a passion for teaching young students
- They are very knowledgeable, and love to convey what they know to others and derive satisfaction in the process
- They love to interact with their students

5
CHAPTER
WHAT IS LEARNING?

LEARNING IS THE PROCESS OF ACQUIRING

- New knowledge and intellectual skills (Cognitive learning)
- New physical skills or manual skills (Psychomotor learning)
- Appropriate emotional responses, attitudes and values (Affective learning)

HOW DO WE LEARN?

- By receiving new knowledge, and
- By processing new knowledge, and retaining it in our mind

RECEIVING NEW KNOWLEDGE

- How do you like to receive the new information? Through sensing or by intuition? (*i.e.*, without any reasoning)
- Through which sensory channel do you perceive external information most effectively? By visual learning or by verbal learning?

PROCESSING NEW KNOWLEDGE

- The way you prefer to process new information
  - ❑ By active learning (by engaging in an activity), or
  - ❑ By reflective learning (learning by a thought process by engaging your mind)
- The way you understand
  - ❑ You want to learn things in a logical sequence? or
  - ❑ You want to learn by forming a mental picture of the entire information
- Study the information given earlier and think of them so that you know about yourself *i.e.*, how do you like to identify yourself?

  Whether you learn

  (*a*) By sensing or by intuition?

  (*b*) By visual means or by verbal means?

  (*c*) By active learning or by reflective learning?

  (*d*) By a sequential process or by thinking of a global picture?
- Answers to the above questions will tell you about your preferred learning style(s)

Improve Your Learning Process

- Observe your learning style .
- Think about what you have observed and about your learning style
- Think about how you can improve your learning process continuously

Characteristics of Good Learners

- Understand your learning process and try to improve your learning process continuously
- Good learners are active (not passive) in their approach to learning process
- Good learners are motivated (*e.g.,* they enjoy learning, they have set short-term and long-term goals).
- Good learners are disciplined (*e.g.,* they follow good study habits and use them consistently)
- Good learners are more aware of themselves (as learners they know their strengths and weaknesses)
- Good learners learn more by utilizing the opportunities available to them (interacting with their colleagues and professors and by reading good text books)
- Good learners set specific learning goals for themselves and work towards achieving the same.
- Expert learners have many learning strategies/styles from which to choose
- Know not only what to learn, but also how to learn (*i.e.,* **"learn to learn"**)
- Systematically plan their approach to learning
- Monitor their learning process while it's happening
- Are more adaptive, because they do self-monitoring while learning
- Think and act, upon their own learning style
- Evaluate the effectiveness of various learning approaches and strategies and choose the best approach
- Desire to achieve their goals by developing their competencies

The Learning Process

Principles of Learning

Carl Rogers (1902-1987) carried out research on learning process, learners and enthusiasms, and has developed a number of principles about how people learn. The principles of learning are:

1. All human beings have a potential for learning.
2. Significant learning takes place when the subject matter is perceived by the learner as having a relevance for his/her own purpose, when the individual has a goal he/she wishes to achieve and sees the material presented to him/her as relevant to the goal, and learning takes place with great ease and quickly.
3. Learning results in self-organization of the subject matter taught.
4. Learning is better when external threats are kept to a minimum.
5. Significant learning occurs by actually doing and by practice.

6. Learning is facilitated when the learner participates responsibly and actively in the learning process.
7. Independence, creativity and self-reliance of the learner are enhanced when self criticism and self-evaluation are carried out by learner himself/herself and evaluation by others is of less importance.
8. The most useful learning in the modem world is the learning of the process of learning (*i.e.*, **learn-to-learn**).

   (Open to experience and to incorporate into oneself the process of change).

Levels of Intellectual Skills as per Bloom's Taxonomy

- Knowledge, knowing and remembering
- Comprehension and understanding
- Applying (Application of concepts, principles and rules)
- Analyzing (Critical analysis, Critical thinking)
- Synthesis (Creating something new, Creative thinking)
- Evaluation and judgement

Asking Questions in the Class

Teachers and Professors may ask different types of questions during the class.

- **Memory level questions (LOTS:** Questions involving Lower Order Thinking Skills)
- **Convergent thinking questions** (All students think and give more or less the same type of answers)
- **Divergent thinking questions** (Students give a variety of possible alternative answers/ solutions which may be considered true or correct)
- **Evaluative thinking questions (HOTS:** Questions involving Higher Order Thinking Skills like critical analysis, critical thinking, creative thinking)

BLOOMS TAXONOMY

Benjamin Bloom created this taxonomy for categorizing different levels of competency to be developed in learning a subject. The taxonomy also provides a useful structure for categorizing test questions.

Competence	Skills Demonstrated	Question Cues		
Lower Order Thinking Skills (LOTS)				
Knowledge	• Observation and recall of information (from memory) • Knowledge of dates, events, places • Knowledge of major ideas • Knowing of subject matter	**List, Define Tell, Describe Identify**	**Show, Label Collect Where Tabulate**	**Quote, Name Who, When**

Contd....

...Contd.

Comprehension	• Understanding information • Grasp meaning • Translate knowledge into new context • Interpret facts, compare, contrast • Order, group, infer causes • Predict consequences	**Summarize** **Describe** **Inerpret** **Contrast**	**Predict** **Associate** **Distinguish** **Estimate**	**Differentiate** **Discuss** **Extend**
Higher Order Thinking Skills (HOTS)				
Application	• Use information • Use methods, concepts, theories in new situations • Solve problems using required skills or knowledge	**Apply** **Demonstrate** **Calculate** **Complete** **Illustrate**	**Show, Solve** **Examine** **Modify** **Relate**	**Change** **Classify** **Experiment** **Discover**
Analysis	• Seeing pattern • Organization of parts • Reorganization of hidden meanings • Identification of components	**Analyze** **Separate** **Order, Infer**	**Connect** **Classify** **Arrange** **Divide**	**Compare** **Select** **Explain**
Synthesis	• Use old ideas to create new ones • Generalize from given facts • Relate knowledge from several areas/disciplines • Predict, draw conclusions	**Combine** **Integrate** **Modify** **Rearrange** **Substitute**	**Plan** **Create** **Design** **Invent** **What If?**	**Compose** **Formulate** **Prepare** **Generalize** **Rewrite**
Evaluation (Judgement)	• Compare and discriminate between ideas • Assess value of theories, presentations • Make choices based on reasoned argument • Verify value of evidence • Recognize subjectivity	**Assess** **Decide** **Rank** **Grade** **Test**	**Recommend** **Convince** **Select** **Judge** **Measure**	**Discriminate** **Support** **Conclude** **Compare** **Summarize**

CHAPTER 6

ATTENDING LECTURE CLASSES

- Each teaching method involves a faculty member who is knowledgeable about a subject (an "expert") communicating what he or she knows to a less knowledgeable person (*viz.,* the student)
- Generally in lectures, most of the communication is one way – *i.e.,* from the teacher to the student

YOU SHOULD KNOW HOW YOUR PROFESSORS ARE TEACHING?

- Your Professors use a variety of teaching styles. Probably lecture method is the most common way by which they teach you
- There are many other methods by which your Professors will also be teaching you

  These are:

  1. Quiz
  2. Role-play
  3. Small Group Discussion
  4. Videos
  5. Games
  6. Use of models and demonstration kits
  7. Cross-word Puzzles
  8. Projects
  9. Questions & Answers sessions
- Whatever method is adopted you should take active part

EDGAR DALE'S CONE OF EXPERIENCE

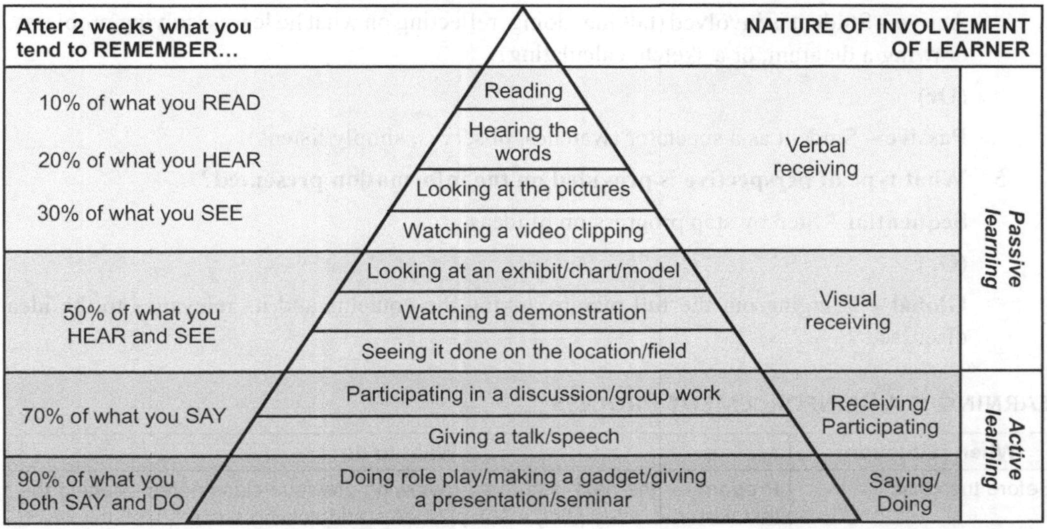

CONE OF EXPERIENCE

Edgar Dale (1900-1985; Ohio State University, Columbus, Ohio, U.S.A) is the Father of Modern Media in Education, developed the "Cone of Experience" from his experience in teaching and his observations of learners.

As you go down the **Cone of Experience,** you are involved in Active Learning by doing the things actually, and in this process you remember/ retain 90% of what you say and do.

Hence you should be more and more involved in activities such as: discussion, group work, group discussion, in giving a speech, doing a role play, fabrication of a device, circuit, system and in giving a seminar/presentation.

OBSERVE HOW INFORMATION IS PRESENTED IN THE CLASS

1. **What type of information is emphasized?**

   Concrete – Facts, data, observable phenomenon

   (Or)

   Abstract – Principles, laws, concepts, theories, mathematical models

2. **What mode of presentation is stressed?**

   Visual – Pictures, diagrams, sketches, video films, demonstrations

   (Or)

   Verbal – Spoken words, words written on the board

3. **How is the presentation organized?**

   Deductive – Start with fundamentals; proceed to applications, state the reasons, proceeding from general to particular

   (Or)

   Inductive – Start with applications; proceed to fundamentals (General inference from particular instance or example)

4. **What mode of student participation is facilitated?**

   Active – Student is involved (talking, doing, reflecting on what he learns, solving problems, drawing a diagram, or a sketch, calculating)

   (Or)

   Passive – Student as a spectator (watches, observes, simply listens)

5. **What type of perspective is provided on the information presented?**

   Sequential – Step by step progression of ideas

   (Or)

   Global – Bringing out the full picture, giving the contents and its relevance to the idea discussed

LEARNING IS A REINFORCEMENT PROCESS

When (Situation)	What to do
Before the class	Prepare for the next lecture by reviewing previous class notes, reading the text material, attempting a few problems and solving some questions which will give you confidence
During the class	Attend the lecture, concentrate on what the teacher does, take detailed notes, ask questions and get your doubts clarified
After the class is over, but before the next class	Review and read the notes, read the relevant text; complete the problems, choose a study partner, if required, or study group to clarify your doubts. If you have doubts, still, meet your teacher and get your doubts clarified
For preparation for class test	Review your notes; review the text, work out the problems, study the important definitions, workout the extra problems and answer the questions in the text
For preparation for final examination	Review notes, read the text, work out the problems, read the assignments given and get your doubts clarified; - prepare memory cards (Cue cards) which contain important definitions, formulae and procedures given by the teacher

CHAPTER 7

MISTAKES STUDENTS MAKE

Mistakes Students Make	Strategies for overcoming them (what you should do to avoid these mistakes?)
1. Assume engineering study will be like studying 10+ 2	Understand and adjust to the differences between 10+2 and engineering study
2. They think they will fail (Losing self-confidence)	Devote adequate time and energy to your studies and develop self-confidence
3. Spend more time outside the campus	Engage yourself in the academic environment of the institution
4. Neglect studying	Devote time and energy for your studies. Think that education is an asset and is an investment for your future.
5. Delay studying until the test in announced	Start studying from the beginning of the Semester. Master the topic of each class prior to next class
6. Trying to study 100% alone by oneself	Study collaboratively with other students also. Engage in group study, it might help you. Study with your friends and classmates.
7. Come to the lecture unprepared	Review class notes, read the text, attempt problems prior to each lecture
8. Avoid talking to Professors	Interact regularly with Professors outside the classroom
9. Cut classes/ don't get the most out of lectures	Attend classes regularly and practice good listening skills. Ask relevant questions in the class and get your doubts clarified.
10. Fail to take notes; or fail to use the notes properly in the learning process	Take notes properly; study the notes and understand the lessons
11. Not reading the text book properly and trying to complete the home work/problems without understanding the steps, procedures or concept(s) involved.	Read' and understand the general concepts before attempting to do the problems
12. Fail to solve the assigned problems	Solve not only the assigned problems but extra problems also. Understand clearly the lesson(s) taught

DON'T HESITATE TO SEEK HELP

Who are the primary sources of "help" for your academic work?

- Your class mates and your friends
- Your professors/teachers

- Your mentor or proctor or students' Counsellor
- Sometimes, a member of your family, parents or a relative might also help you in your academic work

How can you get the most in your College Education?

Students who get the most out of their college education are those:

1. who are more academically involved
2. who organize their study and time effectively
3. who have many inter-personal activities with their faculty members and their fellow students/ classmates
4. who are the happiest in their class

8 CHAPTER IMPORTANCE OF GOOD READING AND COMMUNICATION SKILLS

Just as you learn good behaviour from the examples set by your faculty/professors, you also learn to write and speak in good English by reading the best books and literature.

By reading the world's best books, you can:

- dramatically improve your knowledge of vocabulary
- increase your comprehension skills
- learn to express yourself in an intelligent and concise manner
- improve your power of concentration
- enjoy exciting history/stories from different countries and at various periods of time
- read about the lives and deeds of the world's greatest people, scientists, engineers and philosophers
- develop stimulate your imagination
- improve your ability to think rationally and clearly
- learn to feel for others
- explore the good and evil of human nature, so that you can learn and distinguish the right from the wrong
- take part in discussions about the ideas and beliefs of the world's great thinkers.

These days, it is hard (difficult) to get into the habit of reading, as there are so many distraction while you are studying in the college. Even when books are read, some of them are of a mediocre standard, using a limited vocabulary, colloquial English, slang, incorrect grammar, poor examples of behaviour, as well as dull or depressing plots and shallow characters; Books like this do not teach better standards of English or encourage a higher level of thinking or improve communication skills.

Try to acquire a few of the world's great books and stories, and start reading them; you will slowly gain most, if not all, of the benefits listed above. The more you read, the better your English will become. Don't be scared of reading a book that seems a little difficult at first. It is only by pushing yourself beyond a comfortable limit that you will gain new vocabulary and improve your comprehension and communication skills.

A good way to really appreciate a book, especially one written many years ago, is to find out the approximate year (period) in which the book was written. This will give you an idea about the history of the time, the place, the scientific discoveries made at that time, the politics and philosophy of the era, the clothes being worn, the religion, the food habits and customs of the people/country the book is based on, and information about the author of the book. By doing this, you will understand the book in greater depth and add to your general knowledge as well.

Importance of Reading in your Learning Process

Reading of the class notes and text books is an important activity in the learning process; learning involves many steps and stages:

1. Reading for comprehension and understanding of the subject matter
2. By reading your class notes and text book you begin to understand the theories, definitions, principles, methods and procedures involved in the subject area and thereby gain confidence
3. Reading helps you to solve the problems and to work out the solutions
4. Reading helps you to take up the tests and examinations confidently

Reading for Comprehension and for Understanding the Subject Matter

You should know:

- What to do **before** you read a text book/journal paper.
- What to do **while** you are reading the text matter.
- What to do **after** you read the text matter.

Before You Read

- You should know the purpose of reading
- There are two levels of reading:
  - (*a*) Reading to get a general idea of the subject matter or to have an **overview** of the subject (This is called **superficial reading** or reading at the **surface level** *i.e.,* without going too deep into the subject matter),
  - (*b*) **Reading intensely** to acquire an in-depth knowledge of the subject (*i.e.,* reading for **deeper understanding**).
- Both levels of reading are equally important
- Write marginal notes noting the important ideas as you read the text.
- Make or keep a list of questions and try to answer them after reading the particular topic in the subject.

While You Read

- Read actively. (by concentrating your mind and not distracted by any other idea or thought)
- Try to understand the concepts thoroughly
- Take your own time; don't try to read too fast
- If there is any particular point or portions that you don't understand, make a note of it and get it clarified from your teacher or your friends.
- Periodically, stop and make a mental note of what you have read and understood.

After You Read

- Answer the questions you prepared before you started reading the text or notes
- Read again, a particular portion, if required
- Review everyday what you have read; Review on a weekly basis
- Solve the problems assigned/ Complete the assignment given by the teacher
- Prepare for the test/exam by reviewing the class notes/ text and by solving additional problems (given at the end of the text)
- In some cases, you may have to understand the problem first before you attempt to solve it
- Relate the problem to what you have read earlier and try to solve the problem. Proceed in a logical way, by noting what are the parameters or values given and what is to be found out or solved.

Avoid Procrastination

Procrastination is the habit of postponing the work that we know should be done now itself, but instead we engage ourselves in some other activity.

Reasons for Procrastination

- Fear of failure (*i.e.,* a feeling that work may not be done successfully)
- Fear of success (*i.e.,* the work is done successfully but then what to do next?)
- The work may involve some unpleasant task, which one may not like to do
- The individual is disorganized (*i.e.,* he does not know what to do?)

How to Master the Text Information or your Class Notes?

- Try to learn as much as possible from your lecture notes
- Read the relevant text material and understand the information presented
- Answer the questions given at the end of each chapter in the text book
- Solve the problems given by the teacher and the problems given at the end of each chapter in the relevant text book

How to Learn From Your Class Notes?

- Study and understand the information contained in your notes
- Identify the important definitions, principles, rules or equations and symbols the teacher has explained in the class
- Redraw the sketch or diagram which the teacher has explained in the class
- Try to write a summary of each lecture class. You can refer to the text book but the summary should be written in your own words
- Find the answers to the questions given in the Assignment/Tutorial sheets
- Reflect on (*i.e.,* make a mental picture of) what you have learned
- Review what you have learned on a weekly basis

You should Develop your Communication Skills

- Your communication skills are important in your engineering profession
- Employers want their employees to be good in their communication skills
- Develop a positive attitude about your communication abilities; build on your strengths
- Develop a plan of action to improve your communication skills still further

You should also Improve your Writing Skills to Become a Good Engineering Professional

Good writing skills are required

- In drafting letters, memoranda and e-mail correspondence
- In developing design specifications
- In writing project proposals
- In writing your opinion/comment on a project proposal developed by your colleague(s) or group
- In writing contracts, patents and other interdepartmental documents
- In writing progress reports
- In preparing good technical reports/articles
- For writing and publishing papers in professional engineering journals
- In making evaluation reports of your subordinates

Importance of Oral Communication Skills for an Engineering Professional

- In many instances, you may be required to talk and present about the progress in respect of the work assigned to you/ your team
- You may be asked to present your ideas/views on a new proposal/project
- Will be useful in Project Review and Committee meetings
- In team collaborative work
- Often needed during short courses and in technical training programmes
- Required in Professional Society meetings/Seminars
- Useful in discussing with your subordinates about work related activities

Employers want that Your Communication Skills should be Better and more Effective

A National Survey of over 5,000 engineering employers/ CEO's revealed that industry's concern is:

- Engineering institutions should give their students more instructions and practice in written and oral communications
- This will also improve the employability of the students graduating from engineering colleges

Develop a Strategic Plan to Improve Your Communication Skills

- Take courses/ instructions in oral and written communication
- Look for opportunities to write (keep a record of your important activities briefly describing them); write an essay, article, poem or short story, send e-mails with correct spellings; (reading newspapers, magazines, technical journals and good English novels)
- Develop skill in writing Technical Reports/ Articles
- Look for opportunities to speak in English whenever possible (in Students organizations, Clubs, regular classes, Professional Society meetings)

CHAPTER 9

BALANCE YOUR STUDY/ WORK AND PLAY

- Strike a balance between your immediate and future satisfaction
  - Too much immediate satisfaction – you don't get the work done; you feel guilty
  - Too much delayed gratification – feelings of deprivation and resentment can destroy your commitment
- Find a proper balance between work and play

HOW TO MANAGE YOUR STRESS

- **Eustress** – Positive form of stress; can motivate individuals to attain high level of performance and achievement
- **Distress** – Negative form of stress, can distract you from getting the best
- Attend training sessions on stress management
- Learn strategies for coping up with stress and how to manage stress

GROUP DISCUSSION "IMPORTANCE OF ATTITUDE"

In your group, discuss the following quotation:

"The longer I live, the more I realize the impact of attitude on life. Attitude to me is more important than facts. It is more important than the past, than education, than money, than circumstances, than failures, than successes, than one's appearances, giftedness, or skill. It will make or break a life/ person.

The remarkable thing is we have a choice everyday regarding the attitude we will embrace for that day. We cannot change our past. We cannot change the fact that people will always act in a certain way. We cannot change the inevitable. The only thing we can do is play the one string we have, our attitude.

"I am convinced that life is 10%, what happens to me, and 90% how I react to it. And so it is with you. We are incharge of our Attitudes".

Select a leader amongst your group to lead the discussion on the above topic and keep a record of the important issues discussed and report on what you have learned.

Your Mental and Physical Health is also Important

- Follow tips for good health
- Balance your work and play
- Avoid stress and learn to manage your stress, both physical stress and mental stress

Tips for Good Health

- Eat nutritious food; avoid fast foods (Junk foods)
- Engage in regular physical exercises/activities as far as possible
- Get adequate sleep everyday
- Do not take any medicine without Doctor's prescription/advice
- Avoid alcohol, drugs, tobacco and smoking

Benefits of Daily Physical Activity

- Reduces the risk of heart disease by improving blood circulation throughout the body
- Keeps weight under control
- Improves blood cholesterol levels
- Prevents high blood pressure
- Boosts energy level
- Helps manage stress; Releases tension
- Improves self-image
- Reduces anxiety and depression and increases enthusiasm and optimism
- Increases muscle strength, increases the ability to do physical activities
- Helps build and maintain healthy bones and joints
- Provides a way to share an activity with family and friends
- Establishes good healthy habits and helps to avoid obesity and other undesirable consequences that lead to heart attack and stroke later in life
- Reduces the risk of developing diabetes, colon cancer and many other diseases
- Promotes physical and psychological well-being
- Reduces the risk of dieing prematurely

10

CHAPTER

SEVEN TIPS FOR TIME MANAGEMENT

What you accomplish during a 24-hour period depends on your own motivation, your energy, your skills, talents and abilities, and other resources. Time management is not a way to make you work harder and longer, but a means to help you work smarter to accomplish your work more easily and rapidly.

Here are some strategies you can use to overcome the obstacles that are affecting your time.

1. **Set clear goals for yourself:** You will want to accomplish many things in your life. You must be able to determine what those effective goals are and make sure your efforts are always directed toward their achievement. Effective goals should be : Specific, Measurable, Achievable, Realistic and Time-based. (SMART).
2. **Prioritize:** It is wise to periodically make a list of the tasks that confront you and prioritize them : Determine from the list the things you think are most important to accomplish. A good leader knows when to concentrate on the important and eliminate the rest.
3. **Organise:** As you prioritize tasks and set deadlines, you will want to plan and carryout the activities. Use a planner with a calendar with enough space to make notes for daily activities, contact information, and "to do" lists. You will find this to be an indispensable tool for managing your time. Using a computer also helps in organizing your time.
4. **Being able to say "No" when it is appropriate:** As a leader, you will find you are called on to do much more than you have been asked to do before. When you learn to say "NO" you are not closing the door on your responsibilities, but rather you are making sure that you can meet your commitments and accomplish the maximum possible in the time available to you.
5. **Concentrate on the current task:** Concentration can be difficult when you have a lot on your mind. Your time will be better spent if you are able to focus on your goal and avoid interruptions.
6. **Use your "personal prime time":** Everyone is different. When you plan your tasks, think about your own "prime time" - the time you can concentrate on the more challenging tasks when you are at your best.
7. **Celebrate:** Celebrate the achievement of your goals to maintain a healthy balance in life between work and play. Reward yourself when you complete a task. If you have worked in a team by delegating some tasks to others, reward the efforts of all involved.

Develop a plan to fit your own needs – be flexible to some extent as your needs change.

Learn to Manage Your Time

- Time is precious; you should learn how to manage your time
- Time management will help you to accomplish maximum of your learning everyday and every week, in every semester
- Schedule your time; *i.e.,* allocate time for different activities of your daily routine
- Devote definite time schedules for your daily activities like attending to
  a. Personal needs
  b. For studying in your room
  c. Time for library study
  d. Time for group study, if required
  e. Recreation time with your friends
  f. Time for games, sports and other outdoor activities
- Serious commitment to your scheduled study time is very important

Benefits of Scheduling Your Study Time

- If you have a time schedule you wont feel you are stressed
- Time schedule will help you to keep up with your studies
- It will provide feedback as to how much you are studying and learning everyday or every week
- Within the time period of a day or a week you will know what you can do and cannot do
- If you follow a time schedule, it will give you a feeling that you have more time and that you are relaxed
- If you adhere to your time schedule you will feel that you are not over-stressing yourself during your studies

How many hours you should Devote for your Studies?

This is a tricky question. The answer depends on many factors:

- How difficult is the course?
- How good are you in your studies?
- Some are foundation or core subjects and some are pre-requisite courses for learning other advanced subjects
- What grade do you want to receive?
- During the first semester you may have to spend more time studying preliminary subjects like English, Mathematics, Physics, Chemistry, Engineering Drawing and Computer basics and you are expected to clear them, so that you can devote your time in the subsequent semesters in studying the core engineering subjects of your choice

Making up Your Weekly Schedule

- Identify all your commitments i.e., time for attending theory classes and laboratory classes and time for travel, time for meals etc
- Balance time is available for two purposes
  - For self-study, and
  - For your recreation (extra curricular activities, games, etc)
- Schedule/apportion your study time to avoid wasting time
- What should I study and review on a weekly basis?
- Where should I study?
- What subject(s) should I study?
- How much time I devote for studying each subject?
- These are the questions which you must answer so that you can arrive at a workable time schedule

CHAPTER 11

SELF-STUDY AND GROUP STUDY

- Your learn by yourself *i.e.,* self-study
- You learn with others (It is called **collaborative learning,** as it occurs in a **group study** with one or two of your close friends)
- Identify by which method you learn maximum (You can get your doubts clarified when you study along with your friends, as in group study)
- Both the learning methods, self-study and group-study are equally important

WHY DO STUDENTS STUDY ALONE?

Some of the answers given by students are:

- "I learn more studying by myself"
- "I can study at my own pace and convenience"
- I have my own learning style. Hence I would like to study myself independently
- "I feel group study is a distraction for me/it is a waste of time"
- "I learn very little when I study with my friend(s)"
- "I don't have anyone to study with"

BENEFITS OF GROUP STUDY

However, there are some benefits of Group study:

- You will be better prepared for the world of work when you join an engineering profession. In your work after graduation you may have to work with your colleagues and other engineers, wherein you many have to discuss and understand the job/ task to be done by you and your team
- You will learn more
- Group study improves your inter-personal relationships and communication skills with others
- Your friends can help you to clarify your doubts
- You may enjoy group study more

Self-Study and Group Study

- You should understand that both self-study, and group study are equally useful and important
- What is the ideal size of a study group? Normally it should not be more than 3 or 4 members (of your class)
- What can be done to keep the group from getting off the tasks? (from getting distracted!)
- The group should have an understanding that their main task is to study and learn the subject matter and get the doubts clarified.
- The duration of group study at a time should not be more than 2 to 3 hours in a day

12 CHAPTER

Productive Actions, Positive Thoughts and Positive Feelings

There are two types of actions

1. **Productive actions** – Actions which support the achievement of your goals, aims and aspirations.
2. **Non-productive actions** – Actions which interfere with your profession, work or studies against the achievement of your goals, aims and aspirations.

Value Judgement Applied to your Thoughts

There are two types of thoughts:

- **Positive thoughts** – result in your choosing productive actions and the right actions.
- **Negative thoughts** – result in your choosing non-productive actions, wrong actions or not doing things you are expected or supposed to do or act upon

There are Two Types of Feelings

- **Positive Feelings** – produce positive thoughts, which in turn lead to productive actions and desirable behaviours.
- **Negative feelings** – produce negative thoughts, which in turn lead to non-productive actions; wasteful actions or not doing activities you are supposed to engage in

How to make Behaviour Modification Work for You?

Behaviour Modification

Choose productive behaviours and work to transform negative thoughts to positive thoughts and good feelings and good behaviours will follow.

For realizing success you must follow the three steps strategy:

Step 1: **Acquire Knowledge** – "You know what to do:

Step 2: **Have Commitment** – "You want to do it" and "You have a desire to do it"

Step 3: **Implement New Thoughts or Ideas** – "You actually do it"

Obstacles Faced in Choosing Productive Actions

- You have difficulty in choosing to do things you don't find enjoyable/ easy to implement

- You are afraid to take productive action because you think that if you take the productive action and still fail, it will reflect on your capability and you may lose the confidence
- You prefer to blame your failures on other people or other factors external to yourself

Maslow's Hierarchy of Needs

(1) **Physiological needs:** Food, water, air and shelter

(2) **Safety needs:** Security, orderliness and freedom from fear

(3) **Belongingness:** Feeling of family and friends

(4) **Esteem needs:** Self-respect, achievement, fame and reputation

(5) **Self-Actualization:** To become aware of what you are most fitted for: understanding fully your potentials and working hard to realize your full potentials

What are your "Needs" and "Wants?"

1. *Needs* are things that you must have, things that are essential.
2. *Wants* are things that you desire to have

What is Self-Esteem?

Self-esteem is appreciating one's own worth and importance and having the strength and character to be accountable for one self and to act responsibly towards others

Self-esteem is made up of two components:

(1) **Self-capability** – sense of competence; ability to produce desired effect

(2) **Self-respect** – sense of personal worth and importance

Maslow's Theory of Motivation

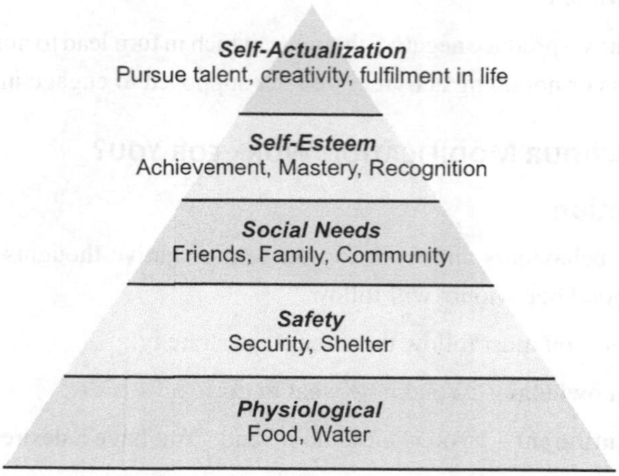

Maslow's (Abraham Maslow; 1908-1970) Hierarchy of Needs identifies five levels of needs, which are best seen as a hierarchy with the most basic need emerging first and the most ultimate need last. People move up the hierarchy one level at a time. Fulfilled needs lose their importance and the next level of needs is activated and strengthened.

Level I – Physiological needs are the most basic human needs. They include food, water and comfort. Physiological needs are satisfied by a regular monthly income.

Level II – Safety needs are the desires for security and stability, to feel safe from any harm. Safety needs are satisfied by having a secured job and a home.

Level III – Social needs are the desires for affiliation. They include friendship and belongingness to the organization and family group. Social needs are satisfied through family get-together, games, sports, parties and celebrations. Social needs are fulfilled by showing concern and care.

Level IV – Esteem needs are the desires for self-respect and respect or recognition from others. Esteem needs are fulfilled by matching the skills and abilities of the person with the job and by appreciating the work done by the person.

Level V – Self-actualization needs are the desires for self-fulfillment and the realization of the individual's full potential. Self-actualization needs are fulfilled by tasks that challenge one's minds consistent with his/her aptitude and training.

Benefits of Knowing your Personality Type and Learning Styles

You should know whether you are:

- An Extrovert or introvert
- Sensing a situation or knowing it by intuition (without reasoning)
  - A Thinking person or a person with more feelings
  - Judging or perceiving (becoming aware of)
- This will help you in selecting the most appropriate engineering job that is suitable for you
- Help you in creating your own learning experiences to meet your needs
- Assist you in appreciating your own uniqueness and strength
- Assist you in appreciating the uniqueness and strength of others in the organization

Understanding Others and Respecting the Individual Differences

- There are differences in personality types and in the learning styles of individuals
- There are cultural, regional and gender differences
- You may have to improve your performance in cross-cultural environment *i.e.,* by communicating and working effectively in a group where people from different cultures, regions and genders work together

You should Draw Up a Personal Development Plan for Yourself

That means you have to

- Identify areas for improvement
- Prioritize them in the order of importance
- Think and create a personal development plan, *i.e.,* an action plan for improving yourself
- Work on them consistently and continuously

CHAPTER 13

Your Personal Growth and Development During your Studies (Co-curricular and Extra-curricular Activities)

- You should be receptive to changes. Strive to change, grow and improve yourself continuously in every area that impacts your study, life and performance effectiveness.
- Your personal development depends on area(s) in which you want to grow, change or develop to achieve your goal.
- Major goal being receiving your B.E/B.Tech Degree in the chosen field of engineering at the end of your studies in the Engineering College.
- In addition, develop knowledge, skills and right attitudes expected from an engineer working in the company, industry, society or in your professional life later.
- Take part in as many co-curricular and extracurricular activities as possible while you are studying in the Engineering College.

Co-curricular and Extracurricular Activities

- Taking part in Co-curricular/Extra curricular activities will help you to broaden the scope of your education in the engineering college
- No one will make you to take part in co-curricular and extra-curricular activities since all these activities are undertaken by the students voluntarily
- These activities will have greater educational value than even your coursework requirements.

Co-curricular Activities

These are:

- Participation in students organizations/clubs
- Participation in engineering projects organized by Institute/College
- Summer training in an industry, Company or Business enterprise
- Taking part in social service activities, community service, Red-Cross activities, road safety week, tobacco/drug awareness camp, NSS (National Service Schedule) activities, blood donation camp etc.,

Types of Students' Organizations

- Students' Chapters of various professional societies
- Participation in literary Clubs/ Associations
- Taking part in Students' Council activities

Organizing and taking parts in Students' Clubs such as:

- Entrepreneurship Club
- Dance Club
- Debating Club
- Dramatics Club
- Fine-arts Club
- Health Club
- Hobby Club
- Movie Club
- Karate Club
- Music Club
- Quiz and G.K Club
- Out-door/ Trekking Club
- Astronomy and Space Club
- Photography Club
- Creativity Club
- Toast-Master Club (for promoting English Speaking Skill)

What are the Benefits of Participation in Students' Organizations?

- It meets your social needs
- It develops your leadership skills and organizational abilities
- It engages you in technical and professional development activities
- It improves your personality traits, communication skills and inter-personal relationships
- Able to participate in students service activities

Benefits of Participation in Engineering Projects at Institutional level or Departmental level

- Students' design competitions are held in engineering colleges and technical institutions. It is important that you take part in these events, as it will add value to your engineering education at the college

- Take part in Technical Paper contests/ Paper presentations
- Design Seminars/ Design Contests
- Take part in undergraduate research. This will help you to know how research project work is carried out in an institutional set-up/ R&D organisations. You may be awarded extra credits for this work. This also helps you to get an exposure in engineering R&D work

Benefits of Industrial Training during your Engineering Studies

- This helps you to develop job related skills
- You can gain exposure to engineering practices/industry standard practices and field practices or business practices
- Apply your knowledge, skills and abilities you have acquired in your studies to practical situations and thereby get work experience which will be useful for your future employment
- Strengthen your motivation to succeed in your studies
- You can get good References (Recommendation letters) for future employment

CHAPTER 14

TEN TIPS FOR SUCCESS IN EXAMINATIONS/TESTS

1. Have a determination that you will learn your subject matter well and pass your examinations.
2. Plan your time (*i.e.* prepare a time schedule) to include periods of study, revision and other commitments–a balance of having games, sports, taking breaks and studying is vital.
3. Use Mind Maps/Concept Maps for your study and for taking notes.
4. Review your notes regularly to reinforce knowledge you have gained.
5. Glance through your text books and course/class notes before you read them in depth to give you an overview of your subject.
6. Learn how to remember lists of things by linking each item logically and by forming a set or grouping of ideas.
7. Before you do any revision, warm up by doing some gentle exercise to relieve any Stress / tension in your body and to get a rush of healthy oxygen flowing to your brain.
8. Do last year question papers as often as possible to familiarize yourself with the type and format of the questions. Keep a note of the time you take for answering these questions.
9. In an examination, make sure you read the question completely and fully understand what the examiner wants before you allocate your time and begin answering the questions.
10. If you are faced with a mental block in answering a particular question breathe deeply, relax and ask yourself "If I did know the answer to this question, what it would be?" Think and write the answer. If you think that you do not have an answer for this particular question, then, go to the next question which you may be able to answer well. Don't get stuck with a particular question, the answer for which you do not know.

A JOURNEY OF A THOUSAND KILOMETERS STARTS WITH ONLY ONE STEP.

GOOD LUCK IN YOUR EXAMINATIONS, AS IT IS THE FIRST STEP OF YOUR SUCCESSFUL CAREER.

PREPARING FOR TESTS/EXAMINATIONS

- Schedule your time for review of lessons you have studied prior to the tests/ examinations
- Revise the portions from your class notes/text book(s)
- Develop practice to perform under time pressure (In some cases, within a short time you may be required to prepare for the examination and do some important work following certain definite guidelines/ steps)

- Get a good night's sleep before your test/ examination
- Make sure you have the right materials and other items for appearing for the tests/ examinations
- Arrive early for the test/ examination

Test-Taking Strategies

- Read/ glance the entire question paper so that you have an overall idea of the test/ examination
- Answer the easier questions first
- Work out the easier problems first
- Be aware of the time available for writing the test/examination
- Allocate the required time for each question, so that you are able to answer all the questions; otherwise you may not have time to write the answers even for easy questions
- Try to complete a problem before leaving it; at the same time be conscious of the time you are taking to solve this particular problem
- Allocate 5 or 10 minutes to check and recheck your answers (never leave a test early)
- Try to write legibly and neatly and don't be careless in answering the questions

Verbs (Words) used in Question Papers and their Meanings

Following are the various directive verbs or words used in the Examination Question Papers. *You should know the meaning of these words so that you can* give the most appropriate answer depending on the scope and nature of the subject:

Analyze	Show the essence of it by breaking it down into its component/ constituent parts and examining each part in detail
Argue	Present the case for and against a particular statement
Compare	Look for similarities and differences between the given statements
Contrast	Discuss the two ideas which are in opposition in order to show the differences between them
Criticize	Give your judgment about the merits or opinions about the idea stated, and support your judgment by discussion
Define	Give the definition as universally stated and accepted. Give the precise meaning of the word, phrase or term.
Describe	Give a detailed information or description giving the important characteristics of the item
Differentiate/ Distinguish	Show the difference(s) between the two items stated
Discuss	Investigate or examine by giving arguments, analyze, giving reasons for and against
Enumerate	Specify and describe the salient points/ features one by one
Evaluate	Make an appraisal of the value of the statement or the idea of its truth or use. Give your personal opinion, supported by evidence
Examine	Check the validity of the statement and comment on it

Explain	Make it clear, interpret, and account for giving details
Explore	Thoroughly enquire by examining and analyzing every aspect of it
Illustrate	Explain clearly by giving concrete examples with figures, diagrams or sketches
Interpret	Bring out the meaning of it clearly and explicitly, also give your own view of it
Investigate	Search, study and critically analyze all aspects of the topic/ problem
Justify	Defend the statement or show adequate proof for your decisions or conclusions
Outline	Give the main points and general principles of the topic omitting minor details, emphasizing structure, sequence and relationship
Prove	Demonstrate whether it is true or false by presenting evidence; establish the relationship based on first principles
Relate	Narrate or show how things are connected to each other and to what extent they are alike or interrelated with each other
Review	Make a survey examining the subject critically
State	Give the precise meaning/definition of the term. Specify details fully and clearly
Sketch	Draw an outline diagram, drawing or figure of the equipment, circuit or process
Summarize	Give a concise account or the important points of the topics, omitting details and examples
Trace	Identify the important milestones/events and describe the development or history of a topic from the beginning or from a particular period/specific instance .

15

CHAPTER

ETHICS

Ethics means right conduct, following righteous path, moral codes, observe standards and norms of society.

Personal ethics consist of honesty, integrity, truthfulness, fairness, etc. *e.g.* giving bribe is an unethical practice

Ethics deals with concern for others. To be ethical means to be truthful, kind, supportive, helpful, sympathetic, fair and encouraging.

Self-interest should not drive individuals to use unfair means to achieve his/her goals. Being ethical means not to steal, bluff, conspire, criticize, betray, hurt, lie; manipulate, falsely accuse and spread rumors.

ACADEMIC INTEGRITY AND ETHICS

Students are expected to attend the classes as scheduled and be prompt in submitting assignments and tutorials. They should not use inappropriate languages in the classroom, offer unwanted remarks, or jokes in class or in the meetings. Students should fulfill in a reasonable way the requirements and expectations of the courses as stated/required by the faculty.

PLAGIARISM (COPYING FROM OTHER'S WORK)

Plagiarism means presenting "ideas, words or statements of another person as one's own without appropriately quoting the source. In assignments/projects you are required to give credit for the ideas of others making a specific point of what you have done and how you have proceeded further with that idea.

Students must perform their work diligently and work ethically. They "must not copy, steal, change, destroy or impede another student's work".

Basic rules and regulations of the institution/library should be followed.

Students must not rip (or tear) pages from journals and books kept in the libraries. They also should not deface any page or portion of the book.

VIOLATIONS OF ACADEMIC INTEGRITY

Academic fraud and dishonesty includes plagiarism, copyright infringement, cheating, fabrication, multiple submission of assignments, obtaining unfair advantage, unauthorized access to academic or administrative systems/ records, aiding and abetting, impersonation and threatening to harm others

1. **Cheating:** Using unauthorized notes, aids, or information in an examination; making alterations in the assignments already graded for any undue advantage. Students should not give his/ her own work/assignments to their friends/ class mates to submit it for grading.
2. **Fabrication:** Giving false information, data, or citation; failing to provide an accurate account of how information, data or citations were gathered; altering documents affecting academic records; forging signatures or making alterations on official academic document, grade sheet, letter, form, ID card, submitting false certificate, giving false excuses for absence, delay or illness
3. **Multiple Submissions:** Submitting identical papers/assignments or course work for credit in more than one course.
4. **Obtaining Unfair Advantage:**
   - Gaining access to examination materials prior to the time authorized by the teacher
   - Stealing, defacing or destroying library or research materials
   - Unauthorized collaboration on an academic assignment
   - Retaining, possessing or circulating previously used examination materials without the faculty's permission
   - Obstructing or interfering with another student's academic work
   - Offering bribe to staff or any university/college employee to effect a grade change, or to gain unfair advantage over other students
5. **Unauthorized Access:** Viewing or altering in any way computer records, modifying computer programmes or systems, releasing or distributing information gathered via unauthorized access, or in any way interfering with the use or availability of computer systems/ information.
6. **Aiding and Abetting:** Providing material, information or other assistance, which violates the Standards for Academic Integrity; providing false information in connection with any inquiry
7. **Impersonation:** Impersonating or allowing to be impersonated by another individual during classes, examination or in other university activities
8. **Threatening to Harm:** Threatening students, doing bodily harm or causing financial loss to any student, faculty, staff or administrator
9. **Misconduct:** Behaving in a manner that violates or adversely affects the rights of other students or members of the academic community (disrupting class/campus activities, unruly behavior etc.,)
10. **Copyrights Infringement:** Using copyright materials (print material, non-print material, software, electronic, or multimedia) in a manner that violates copyright laws
11. Students should not indulge in any theft or damage of the university/college property

Code of Ethics for Engineers

Code of Ethics describes ethical responsibilities and obligations for individuals and institutions, both academic and corporate. The Code is indicative of the expectations of academic and professional behaviour, of teachers and faculty.

The Code of Ethics is applicable to educators and industry partners also who work with them, occupy positions of significant authority, and that authority is accompanied by significant ethical responsibilities. Engineers who perform professional work in an engineering/technical discipline are bound by the Code of ethics of their respective professional society, including adhering of standards concerning safety, health and welfare of the public.

1. Ensure that all students have an understanding of their professional and ethical responsibilities.
2. Encourage students to use their knowledge and skills for the enhancement of safety, health and human welfare.
3. Encourage students to become aware of the environment and social impact of their decisions and engineering solution they provide.
4. Improve their expertise by continuing professional development and provide such opportunities for colleagues also.
5. Undertake professional work and responsibilities only in the areas of their expertise and competence.
6. Be honest and impartial, with no tolerance for bribery, fraud, corruption and academic dishonesty, and instill these principles in their students.
7. Respect the intellectual property of others by properly crediting and giving reference to their previous works and sharing appropriate credit with coauthors, including students, if any.
8. Avoid actual or apparent conflicts of interest.
9. Build the students professional reputations on the merit of their own work.
10. Treat all persons without any prejudice regardless of religion, gender, disability, age, or national origin.
11. Show respect for students and professional colleagues, never tolerating harassment.
12. Protect confidential information concerning students and professional colleagues.
13. Provide fair evaluation of students and professional colleagues that reflect the true merit of their work.
14. Support other professional colleagues to follow this code of ethics.

(* Adapted from ASEE, Prism, Vol. 22, No. 3, Nov. 2012, pp 55)

16

CHAPTER

Employment Opportunities and Job Search

How do you identify your Employment Opportunities

- Look for announcements by your Placement and Training Department/ Division for potential campus interviews
- Attend on-campus interviews;
- Use the internet and apply on-line
- Check other sources of employment
- Consult your professors, teachers and seniors to help you in your job search
- Read "opportunities" column/section published by newspapers

How do you Conduct a Job Search?

- Prepare a Resume/Curriculum Vitae (your certificates and other credentials)
- Prepare a covering letter
- Develop your interviewing skills
- Identifying various employment opportunities available
- Contact your Placement and Training Officer/Department for counselling and for guidance.

How do your Employers measure your Potential when they Interview you for a Job?

- Your academic performance in the School and 10+2 class
- Your academic performance in the Engineering College
- Your achievements in co-curricular and extra- curricular activities
- Your personal qualities and talents
- Your References/Letters of recommendation from your professors, teachers and company executives in whose industry you did project work/industrial training
- Your performance during the interview
- Your attitude towards your work

CORE COMPETENCIES (SOFT SKILLS) EMPLOYERS LOOK FOR IN RECRUITING ENGINEERS AND MANAGERS

- **Innovation**

  (Capable of generating new and unique ideas)
- **Decision Making**

  (Selects the best course of action from amongst several feasible alternatives)
- **Self-Awareness and Self-assessment**

  (Ability to learn about one self and recognize one's own strengths and weaknesses)
- **Drive and Enthusiasm**

  (Highly motivated bubbling with zeal and interest)
- **Interpersonal Relationships**

  (Ability to express and communicate so as to maintain cordial relationship)
- **Strategic Thinking**

  (Developing a creative solution combining own ideas with others)
- **Resilience and Endurance**

  (Ability to work under pressure)
- **Valuing Others Ideas**

  (Making certain that others get their due credit for their ideas)
- **Collaboration with Others**

  (Promoting team work and team spirit)

17

CHAPTER

Professional Skills

You are expected to possess and continuously develop the following professional skills:

1. Introducing yourself (Creating a positive impression)
2. Listening – Understanding what people say
3. Listening – Showing interest in people
4. Communicating your feelings (positively)
5. Dealing with anger/hostility
6. Responding to praise
7. Responding to expression of anxiety
8. Responding to negative feedback
9. Coping with apathy and expressions of disinterest
10. Coping with silence during conversations
11. Appreciating others people's feelings
12. Giving information correctly
13. Simplifying complex information
14. Advising on emotional issues/difficulties
15. Seeking clarification
16. Asking open-ended questions
17. Waiting for replies
18. Changing direction or trend of conversation
19. Expressing support to others
20. Self-disclosure of personal information as appropriately required
21. Making a conversation more serious
22. Making a conversation less serious
23. Summarizing what people have said
24. Holding someone's interest and attention
25. Ending conversation in a positive way
26. Organizing skills for carrying out a given task

27. Skills in Time management
28. Liaising with others
29. Resolving conflicts and misunderstanding
30. Developing self-confidence
31. Making a conversation a pleasant experience

21st Century Skills

While you are studying in the Engineering College, it is expected that you learn and acquire 21st Century Skills, in addition to acquiring technical competencies in you chosen professional field. These skills are:

- Learning to know
- Learning to live together
- Learning to do, and
- Learning to be

The 21st century learning encompasses the skills that are significant and important for you to acquire:

- Collaboration – the ability to work in cross functional team(s)
- Critical thinking – taking on complex problem
- Oral communications – presenting the information
- Written communication – through writing assignments
- Technology – use of Information and Communication Technology (ICT)
- Learn about careers – through internships and industrial training
- Citizenship – take on civil and global issues and learning through active community service

18

CHAPTER

Attributes of Good Leadership

- Self-Control
- Keen Sense of Fairness and Justice
- Good Decision Making
- Good Planner (Plan his work and Work his plan)
- Willingness to do more than what is just required
- Pleasing Personality
- Sympathetic and Good Understanding
- Masters details
- Willingness to Assume Full Responsibility
- Cooperate
- Exhibits Confidence and Courage

21 Indispensable Qualities of a Leader; (Courtesy: John Maxwell, Leadership Outline)

1. **Character** (good qualities and features)
2. **Charisma** (powerful personal quality that attracts other people)
3. **Commitment** (promise to do)
4. **Communication** (process of expressing ideas and feelings)
5. **Competence** (ability to do well)
6. **Courage** (bravery/opposing without showing fear)
7. **Discernment** (ability to show good judgement)
8. **Focus** (give attention to one particular thing)
9. **Generosity** (willing to give more than what is necessary)
10. **Initiative** (ability to decide and act on your own)
11. **Listening** (paying attention to what you hear)
12. **Passion** (strong feeling of love/enthusiasm)

13. **Positive Attitude** (positive way of thinking and feeling)
14. **Problem Solving** (finding a solution/finding ways of dealing with problems)
15. **Relationships** (ways in which people behave towards each other)
16. **Responsibility** (taking care of)
17. **Security** (activities involved in protecting)
18. **Self-Discipline** (ability to make yourself do)
19. **Servanthood** (ability to render service with devotion)
20. **Teachability** (able to learn by being taught)
21. **Vision** (ability to think about/plan the future with great imagination and intelligence – foresight)

YOUR MANAGEMENT STYLE

Important characteristics of good leaders and their management style (Courtesy: "Quality is Free" by Philip B. Crosyby, 1979)

These are :

- Importance of Listening
- Cooperating and Team Work
- Helping others
- Communicating
- Creating (Be creative)
- Implementing a solution
- Learning (Be a life long learner)
- Leading Others, and
- Following the Leader

There are other important characteristics like integrity and compassion. These are vital and fundamental facts of one's character, they cannot be learned or vastly improved from without, but you cannot succeed in the company or business without them. As a matter of fact it is difficult to think of any profession you would want to be part of that wouldn't demand a great deal of integrity and compassion.

If you want to accomplish more than what you have accomplished in this complex world you have to be more than the next person. Take advantage of the assets you have.

IMPORTANCE OF LISTENING

You can pay people no greater honour than to actually absorb the content and intent of what they have to say. Not just the message as you have heard superficially; but you must concentrate on what is said behind the words. Listen really to the speaker. Is the person in trouble? Does he/she want help? Is he/she saying one thing and meaning another? What is really going on?

You must listen and question until you are sure you understand the message. You will discover an interesting world. Once people find that you are willing to take the time to understand them, they will take the time to arrange thoughts into concepts that are easier for you to comprehend. You may even create some listeners of your own. Then you can reach a state where true communication takes place. You are actually transmitting, and receiving, real meanings.

Once you have a basis for eliminating or preventing misunderstandings, success is at hand. Nothing is more important than true understanding.

Cooperating and Team Work

Being part of a team is not a natural instinct or human function; it is learned. Participants in a contact sport, such as football or hockey learn quickly that the rest of the team evaluates personal worth by evaluating a team member's determination to cooperate. The player must not only makes the play to be executed and successful, but protect others as well in the process.

To cooperate with others in accomplishing a task is one of our nobler achievements. It is also one of the more productive aspects of the manager with a style. The whole really is greater than the sum of its parts. Synergism really does work, if you take care of it.

Cooperation doesn't mean that you have to abandon or sacrifice any of your personal traits or standards. You can leave one team and join another. Make certain that the team is worthy of you, just as you must be worthy of the team. Expect only the best. Don't settle for less. A sure way to successful cooperation is to help build a winning team from one that is not doing well. Bring people together, manage and lead. The same principles apply in relationships with individuals. Those who are known to work with others for a common goal become known as trustworthy people.

But most of all, do not be uncooperative. If that is so, you will be ignored. Ignored managers cannot cooperate with anyone.

Helping Others

Helping and cooperating are not the same. Helping involves giving, without direct expectation of immediate return. It is letting someone lean on you without getting to lean back. In cooperating you are both, together, learning on something for mutual support.

In corporate life, helping has to do with smoothening the road for others, whether they know you are doing it or not. It is being available when someone needs help, it is putting in a good word for some one who deserves it. It is like offering a discrete personal loan or gift without making a big deal out of it.

To help in a positive manner, you must be genuinely interested in people and results. True help is truly unselfish. You must have the patience to wait until the individual recognizes that he/she really does need assistance. Help must be carefully thought out. If you are prepared to offer assistance properly, you can guide him and counsel him as well. If you are confident that your efforts to help are based on a genuine concern for the individual, and are not to further your own ends, then the help will be accepted.

Communicating

Techniques such as public speaking, personality improvement courses/sessions, transactional analysis, appropriate and effective use of body language-these and many other activities have been undertaken by people in the hope of improving the way they communicate.

Usually they achieve a better understanding of themselves, which is what most of these activities are all about, but they fail to improve their communication. They don't understand or believe a fundamental truth you have to have something to say.

"Communicating" is a characteristic functional activity because there is much more to conversing your thoughts than just "speaking". Your dress/clothes, your physical manner, your personality, your cleanliness and many other things transmit a lot about you, often so loudly and cleanly that the words you choose to say may not be heard, at all. How are you communicating should not be left, to chance.

These are three basic communicational actions : Writing, prepared speaking, and conversation.

(*a*) **Writing** is putting one's thoughts clearly, short and direct (straight); long and drawn out message is undesirable. Writing helps you bring your thoughts together coherently so that others can understand them. You may be struggling continuously to make yourself understood. Writing is the hardest in the art of communication. When you speak to an audience, you can get a little feedback as you go along. You can detect confusion, boredom, or drowsiness. Reading is a private act, and you can never know if someone understands what you have written unless that person shows evidence of having understood (or misunderstood). Being understood is hard work. But, if you are successful at it, you can achieve more than you ever dreamed.

(*b*) **Prepared Speaking** is a rewarding communication method; and it takes a lot of efforts. But a really good speech doesn't seem well prepared, and yet it takes so long to produce one. Preparing formally for any speech is always desirable. Training programmes on effective public speaking are regularly organized for faculty/employees in the organsiation/institution. In addition, professional help is advised for learning how to construct a good speech and this gives confidence.

(*c*) **Conversation:** Many people feel that conversation requires no preparation and attention. Smart executives, engineers and managers listen to themselves and learn how to improve. They learn things like how important it is to look into the eyes of the other person; like when to touch them and when not; like when not to be clever or funny; like when just to remain silent.

All these communication factors, such as writing, speaking and conversing project a picture of you on everyone's mental wall, what they see is what they think you are. You may feel that you are something else, and may actually not be what is being projected to others.

Creating (Be creative)

You should learn to be creative. You can create solutions to complicated problems by being the only one to break that complicated problem down to its basic elements/causes. Once these causes are exposed, a creative solution appears - if you can recognize it. Unfortunately, many people give up before that. New and original solutions are a result of hard work.

Problem solving is an acquirable skill; many techniques and concepts for learning creativity are available. The most practical technique, however, is to go and ask the people who are involved with the problem on the job/shop floor; not the management people (like engineers/managers), but the working people i.e. people on the job. The operators are delighted that someone cares about their opinion. They share with you to create a solution. At the same time, make certain, that they also get their due credit.

One other source of creativity is to expand on the ideas of others, or to work on the old ideas and update them. Give credit where it is due.

Don't tell that you lack creative activity. Everyone is endowed with creativity which can be nurtured and developed.

Implementing a Solution

The most valuable manager is one who can first create and then implement. You can implement others ideas/concept also or add your own improvements to already existing methods. Most managers can only follow directions; but real implementers are appreciated and are respected by others.

You have to get the job done. Understanding the basic problems, determining a practical solution, convincing others about the new solution, and then getting it done is the way to move forward. Many quality/productivity improvements are like that. Don't expect commitment that every one will cooperate. If you can get it is wonderful.

Learning (Be a Life Long Learner)

Learn your subject. The more information you have about everything, especially people, technology and finance, the more you can accomplish. When you have an answer for everything, you have stopped learning. Hence, it is essential, that you should not stop learning. It is important that you read new information and listen. Read at least a few magazines/books every week or month. Don't follow the same routine. Keep yourself alive.

It is not always possible to know what you need to learn. Therefore, you have to constantly seek out new experiences and exposures. You should know the latest developments; know how to deal with them or the effect they create. Relate the new developments to those of the past. New activities are stimulating and challenging; they exercise the learning muscles in you continuously. It will create positive feelings and thoughts and enthusiasm in you.

Leading Others

Leaders communicate by giving clear and unambiguous direction and by setting examples as evident. Leading means stating the objectives in a clear way that is precisely understood, ensuring commitment of individuals to those objectives, defining how the results will be measured and then by providing impetus to get things done. Leading is a hard and unending job. To lead, you have to keep everyone busy. The leader should never run out of ideas/jobs, for the people who are working under him and seeking his guidance.

The conventional thoughts about the problems of being a leader: the long hours, the problems of choosing between those who are coming up and those who are going down. Leader has to survive such problems.

Leaders' great mistake is the belief that only they can set the goal, their belief that they know how to do anything.

Open-mindedness-an approach in which ideas are floated, widely discussed and guidelines are proposed openly- is the only cure. A closed leadership doesn't grow. Solo shows are also not conducive for good leadership.

Following (The Leader)

It is not easy to be a good follower. A good follower wants the same results that the leader wants. The follower doesn't necessarily need to have identical goals, but the desire for the same results must exist.

A good follower takes time to make certain that he or she understands the intent (intention) of the leader's request as well as his words. Good followers, who want to expand their sphere of influence, get promoted and move into higher activities. They expand into an area where there is a lot of scope to act and do it with the full understanding of the leader. They de not compete with the leader. Be a good follower, leading will take care of itself.

19 CHAPTER CREATIVITY

Creativity in the workplace must be nurtured and cultivated for it to flourish. This means creating a culture of trust and having the freedom to express new ideas without being ridiculed, allowing room for mistakes, and developing the vision to spot opportunities in unexpected places.

CREATIVITY AND INNOVATION

'Creativity' is the process of generating new ideas or concepts, or even devising new ways in which already existing ideas and concepts can be combined. Thus, creativity is a thought process, a fertile thought process.

'Innovation', on the other hand, is the conversion of these creative ideas and concepts into commercially viable products or processes that meet specific organizational goals.

Creativity and Innovation are not separate entities, they in fact go together: Creativity without innovation renders the so called idea useless in the absence of its transformation to new products or process.

In the present context of today's events, creativity and innovation should be viewed as a continuous improvement process of devising new ways and products. Innovation and Research would play a key role in the future.

Characteristics of Innovative Leaders:

- Fast and action oriented.
- Deeply immersed and involved in progressive changes.
- Future – obsessed.
- They are highly motivating and inspiring.
- Passionate about their dreams and goals.
- They don't take "No" for an answer.
- They are Institution and Organization Builders.
- High-gain and risk-takers; they don't think small. Their plans are always grandiose; they think big and their actions are daring.

Innovative leadership is the highest form of leadership because of the positive impact and huge contributions they have made in the lives of their engineers, employees, customers and community. Innovative leaders take their companies and organizations to far greater heights and to exciting destinations.

We need innovative leaders who can transform the people they lead, transform the people they interact within their organizations. The people, then, go on to transform the business landscape and, thus, the entire organization.

Innovative leadership calls for challenging current processes, envisioning a change, developing and inspiring a share vision, and modeling and leading the way forward. These leaders have charisma, have vision, propagate intellectual stimulation, and above all inspire people across all disciplines.

PEOPLE SKILLS

An independent study by Stanford Research Institute and Carnegie Mellon University, U.S.A. on CEOs, who are indisputable leaders of their organizations, revealed that long term success depends 75% on people skills and 25% on technical skills. Another research by Harvard University U.S.A. found that organizations lose 10-15% of their business due to the lack of soft skills in their employees. Innovative leaders need to take cognizance of this fact.

Who is a "A Team Player"?

It is very difficult to describe a team player. We look for intellect and personality, but we also look for internal qualities like motivation, creativity and drive. We want people with a desire to win, who can leaverage their own talents as part of a team, not some one who is focused on pursuing individual achievement. It is difficult to list the right combination of adjectives. You can see it in athletes. The best foot ball players are not necessarily the fastest.

Product Innovation and Product Leadership

Product innovation and product leadership are two important ingredients for a company to become successful. Michael Tracy in his book: **"Discipline of Market leaders"** talks about **three different strategies : "product leadership", "cost leadership"** (operational efficiency) and **"customer intimacy"**. Continuous innovation is necessary in the global economy. Many successful companies have embraced product leadership from day one, with a high degree of customer intimacy.

An innovative leader simply achieves excellence in a different way than he once envisioned. Instead of working his way up an existing ladder, he is building a new one.

Advise for young future business leaders:

Do what you love, and choose your people well and wisely. Great people, will help any leader to achieve great things.

"The 21st century illiterate is not the one who cannot read nor write, but the one who cannot learn, unlearn, and relearn" (Alvin Toffler, World's most famous futurologist).

INNOVATION STRATEGIES

1. Think out-of-box
2. Think laterally (learn to think differently)
3. Develop and Cultivate Creativity
4. Acquire new skills and talents
5. Look for new patterns and value creations
6. Consider "Problems" as "Challenges"
7. Convert the "Challenges" into "Opportunities"

8. Dare to be different
9. Challenge the "Status quo", no matter how perfect the "Status quo" is
10. Have "Fire in the Belly" to convert ideas into reality
11. Develop a Passion for Excellence
12. Unshackle the human spirit of Creativity
13. Minimize the innovation cycle time
14. Maximize the innovation success rates
15. Be competitive
16. Convert the "Constraints" into "Advantages"
17. Learn from failures
18. Foster high performance work culture

12 Engineering Innovations

(1) The Computer	:	Changed the way world WORKS
(2) The Microphone	:	Changed the way world SPEAKS
(3) The Telephone	:	Changed the way world COMMUNICATES
(4) The Electric Bulb	:	Changed the way world SEES
(5) The Radio	:	Changed the way world BROADCASTS
(6) The Airplane	:	Changed the way world FLIES
(7) The Television	:	Changed the way world is ENTERTAINED
(8) The Rocket	:	Changed the way world EXPLORES
(9) The Barcode	:	Changed the way world IDENTIFIES
(10) The Laser	:	Changed the way world uses LIGHT
(11) The Mobile Phone/ The Cell Phone	:	Changed the way world COMMUNICATES on the move
(12) The World Wide Web	:	Changed the way world CONNECTS

Top 11 Technologies of the Decade

No.1	Smart phones
No.2	Social Networking
No.3	Voice Over IP
No.4	LED Lighting
No.5	Multi-core CPUs
No.6	Cloud Computing
No.7	Drone Aircraft
No.8	Planetary Rovers
No.9	Flexible AC Transmission (FACT)
No.10	Digital Photography
No. 11	Class-D Audio

20 CHAPTER

Importance of Problem Solving in Engineering and Technology

The engineering profession requires engineers to deal with uncertainty and solve complex problems from the world of work and society, sometimes with incomplete information/data. In addition, engineers need to be able to function as effective members of the inter-displinary team(s) and have strong problem-solving and communication skills. Today's engineering graduates need to develop these skills and apply their fundamental knowledge for solving problems of society and work place.

Problem Solving

"Problem Solving" need not be confined only to solving numerical problems in mathematics, science, engineering or technology related courses. It can be applied even to learn a new language, which is known as "Linguistic Problem Solving". Research studies in this area have shown that first **"understanding"** occurs and then **"learning"** is demonstrated.

Present day engineers need to develop new skills involving developing the right habits, abilities, thoughts, ideas and technical mastery. Practical wisdom of knowing the task and carrying it out to solve a problem is equally important.

A problem is a situation, condition, or an issue that remains unresolved and makes it difficult to accomplish a desired objective. The situation, condition or issue is considered as a problem when an individual or a group become aware of the significant difference between what is desirable and what is actually the situation. Trying to find a solution or an answer to a problem is known as problem solving. The "problem" in this context need not be confined to "numerical question(s)" only as normally understood in science and engineering courses. It can be any situation, condition or an issue which needs to be resolved. The very nature of engineering discipline is the application of theory to solve problems. This idea needs to be inculcated in the students from semester one.

Problem solving is an hierarchical process by which a situation is analysed, workable solution arrived at and corrective action is implemented. The strategic steps involved are:

- **Defining** the problem (clarifying the situation, condition or issue)
- **Analyze** causes
- **Generate/Identify** alternatives/ideas
- **Assess** the alternatives in terms of its pros and cons
- **Select/decide** the most feasible alternative (solution)

- **Identify** the steps required to implement the solution
- **Implement** the solution, and
- **Evaluate** whether the problem is solved or not

Problem Solving Techniques

There are many problem-solving techniques:

- Affinity Diagrams (organizing ideas into a common theme)
- Ansoff Matrix (understanding different risks/implications of different alternatives)
- Appreciating (understanding information extracted from facts)
- Appreciative Enquiry (looking at what is going right and solving the problems)
- Brain storming (generating a large number of ideas to solve a problem)
- Cause and Effect Diagrams (identifying possible causes of problems)
- Critical Success Factors (identifying critical factors that really matter for success)
- Five Whys Technique (quickly getting to the root of a problem)
- Flowcharts (understanding how a process works)
- Lateral Thinking (changing/inversing the concepts and perception)
- Reframing Matrix (examining problems from distinct viewpoints)
- Systems Analysis (identifying the various factors and understanding how they interact with and affect one another), and
- Root Cause Analysis (identifying the various factors of problems or events)

During the course of your engineering study, many of these techniques will be taught by your professors in the respective subjects.

21 CHAPTER

INTERNET INFORMATION SOURCES

Today Internet and its related technologies like www. have resulted in the rapid proliferation of electronic information. No innovation in history has so profoundly changed our lives as the Internet. Information Resources available on Internet are:

1. **google.com** Google enables users to search the information, including web pages, images and videos. Offers unique features and search technology.
2. **yahoo.com** is a major internet portal and service provider offering search results, customized content, chatrooms, free e-mail, clubs, and pager.
3. **Wikipedia.org** is a multilingual, web-based, free-content encyclopedia project based on an openly editable model. Wikipedia's articles provide links to guide the user to related pages with additional information.
4. **amazon.com** is a customer-centric company, where customers can find and discover anything they might want to buy online, and endeavors to offer its customers the lowest possible prices.
5. **facebook.com** is a social network that connects people, to keep up with friends, upload photos, share links and videos.
6. **youtube.com** is a way to send your videos to the concerned people. Upload, link and share your videos worldwide.
7. **Twitter.com** is a social networking and micro-blogging service utilizing instant messaging, SMS or a web interface.
8. **linkedin.com** is a networking tool to find connections to relevant persons, industry experts and business partners. Allows registered users to maintain a list to contact details of people they know and trust in business.
9. **ebay.com** is an International person-to-person auction site, with products sorted into categories.
10. **alibaba.com** is an import and export trade connections and opportunities.
11. **flicker.com** is picture galleries available with chat, groups, and photos.
12. **aks.com** offers search for web sites, images, news, blogs, video, maps and directions, local search and shopping.

13. **skype.com** is a peer to peer internet voice service. Mac, Windows and Linux versions are available. Users may call landlines and cell phones for a fee; users may call each other for free.
14. **dropbox.com** stores, synchronizes and shares files online with public access. It provides a desktop client for Windows, Mac, and Linux.
15. **thefreedictionary.com** offers English, Medical, Legal and Computer dictionaries, Thesaurus, Encyclopedia, a Literature Reference Library, and a Search Engine all in one.
16. **Naukri.com** India's No.1 job site and the flagship brand of Info Edge revolutionized the concept of recruitment in India. Naukri.com is a recruitment platform that provides employment related services to corporate/recruiters, placement agencies and to jobseekers in India and overseas.
17. **braintrack.com** is an higher education and career resource with worldwide reach. It features a directory of the world's universities and colleges with over 10,000 institutions listed from over 190 countries. The site is the largest directory of universities and colleges on the Web. Brain Track's goal is to help individuals to make better decisions about their education and careers.

22

CHAPTER

QUOTABLE QUOTES

- To awaken interest and kindle enthusiasm is the sure way to **teach** easily and effectively.

  — Tryon Edwards
- Miles to go before I sleep

  — Robert Frost
- Life is like riding a bicycle,

  To keep your balance, you must keep moving

  — Albert Einstein
- The art of **teaching** is the art of assisting discovery

  — Mark Van Doren
- A **Professor** is a person who enters a College and never leaves it.
- Tell me and I forget,

  Teach me and I remember,

  Involve me and I learn

  — Benjamin Franklin
- Behind every successful **student** lies an "exhausted" **teacher**
- In **teaching** you cannot see the fruit of a day's work. It is invisible and remains so, may be for many years.

  — Jacques Barzun
- **Teaching** kids to count is fine,

  But **teaching** kids "what" counts is best

  — Bob Talbert
- He who struggles is better than he who never attempts.

  — Swami Vivekananda
- It is the supreme art of the **teacher** to awaken the joy in creative expression and knowledge.

  — Albert Einstein
- Creativity is a natural extension of our enthusiasm.

  — Earl Nightingale

- Be a wonderful role model.
  Because you will be the window
  Through which many children will see their future

— Thomas Mekinnon

- A mediocre **teacher** tells,
  A good **teacher** explains
  A superior **teacher** demonstrates and
  A great **teacher** inspires

— William Arthur Ward

- The secret of **education** lies in respecting the **student**

— Ralph Waldo Emerson

- The important thing in life is not the triumph but the struggle

— Pierre de Conbertin

- Ideal **teachers** are those who use themselves as bridges over which they invite their **students** to cross, then having facilitated their crossing, joyfully collapse, encouraging them to create bridges of their own.

— Nikos Kazantzakis

- **Teaching** is the royal road to **learning**.

— Jessamyn West

- I like the teacher who gives you something to take home to think about besides homework

— Lily Tomlin

- One of the best ways to persuade others is to **listen** intensely to them

— Geottrey Moss

- What nobler employment, or more valuable to the state than that of the man who **instructs** the rising generation.

— Marcus Tullius Cicero

- Who dares to **teach** must never cease to learn!

— John Cotton Dana

- You can't **teach** a man anything;
  You can only help him discover it in himself

— Galileo Galilei

- If the facts don't fit the theory, change the facts

— Albert Einstein

- Education is when you read the fine print,
  Experience is what you get if you don't

— Pete Seeger

- "Education gives you Knowledge,
  but Life teaches you Wisdom to
  succeed in your professional career"
- In matters of principle, stand like a rock;
  In matters of taste, swim with the current.

— Thomas Jefferson

- In the future, "illiteracy will not be defined by those who cannot read and write, but by those who cannot learn and relearn"

— Alvin Toffler : the Futurist

- Obstacles are those frightful thing you see when you take your eyes off your goal

— Henry Ford

- Put your heart, mind, intellect and soul even to your smallest acts. This is the secret of success
- It is impossible to excel at something you don't enjoy
- Striving for success without hard-work is like trying to harvest where you haven't planted
- Patience, Persistence and Perspiration
  make an unbeatable combination for success
- There are no secrets to success
  It is the result of preparation, hard work, and
  Learning from failure
- Never regard study as a duty, but as the enviable opportunity to learn.
- Success is the sum of small efforts, repeated day in and day out.
- Success is getting things done efficiently, getting the results, you want, and being at peace with yourself and others at the same time.
- Strength doesn't come from physical capacity. It comes from an indomitable will.
- The reward for work well done is the opportunity to do more.
- Doing what you **like** is **freedom**;
  Liking what you do is **happiness**
- Genius begins great works;
  Labour alone finishes them
- If your actions inspire others
  to dream more, learn more, do more
  and become more, you are a Leader.
- When I give a lecture, I accept that people look at their watches, but what I do not tolerate is when they look at it and raise it to their ear to find out if it has stopped.

— Marcel Achard

- Time is the scarcest resource; and unless it is managed, nothing else can be managed.

— Peter Drucker

- "If you can't explain it simply, you don't understand it well enough".

—Albert Einstein

- Imagination is more important than knowledge

— Albert Einstein

- It is the supreme art of the teacher to awaken joy in creative expression and knowledge.

— Albert Einstein

- What I hear, I forget; What I see, I remember, What I do, I understand.

— Confucius

- Education is an ornament in prosperity and a refuge in adversity.

— Aristotle

- The roots of education are bitter, but the fruit is sweet.

— Aristotle

- You must be the change you wish to see in the world

— Mahatma Gandhi

- The art of teaching is the art of assisting discovery.

— Mark Van Dorn

- The most important thing in communication is to hear what isn't being said

— Peter Drucker

- A lamp cannot light another lamp, unless it itself is lit.

— Rabindranath Tagore

- I cannot teach anybody anything. I can only make them think

— Socrates

- Genius is 1% inspiration and 90% perspiration

— Thomas Alva Edison

- The mediocre teacher tells. The good teacher explains. The superior teacher demonstrates. The great teacher inspires.

— William Arthur Ward

- A teacher cannot truly teach unless he himself is learned
- Be a good listener. Listening shows caring and makes the other person feel important
- Never change your originality because no one can play your role better than you. So be yourself and be original.
- No person can be great leader unless he takes genuine joy in the success of those under him.
- Be a positive thinker, even a stopped watch is right twice a day

- Science is organized knowledge; Wisdom is organized life.
- The height of candles may differ, but, they yield the same brightness. It is not the matter of your position but your ability that shines.
- There are three kinds of people in the world; one who makes things happen, one who watch things happen, and one who wonder what has happened.
- Winners don't do different things; but they do things differently.
- Yesterday is history, tomorrow is a mystery, today is a gift, that's what we call it the present.
- It's all to do with the training; you can do a lot if you're properly trained.

— Elizabeth II (The Queen of England)

- Instruction ends in the classroom, but education ends only with life.

— F. W. Robertson

- We cannot teach people anything; we can only help them discover it within themselves.

— Galileo Galile

- Knowing is not enough; we must supply. Willing is not enough; we must do.

— Goethe

- For learning to take place with any kind of efficiency students must be involved; To be motivated, they must become interested. And they become interested when they are actively working on projects which they can relate to their values and goals in life.

— Gus Tubeville

- Some are born with knowledge, some derive it from study, and some acquire it only after a painful realization of their ignorance.

— Confucius

- "Before you become too entranced with gorgeous gadgets and mesmerizing video displays, let me remind you that information is not knowledge, knowledge is not wisdom, and wisdom is not foresight. Each grows out of the other, and we need them all".

— Arthur C. Clarke

- Education is what survives when what has been learned has been forgotten.

— B. F. Skinner

- Genius without education is like silver in the mine.

— Benjamin Franklin

- The only person who is educated is the one who has learned how to learn and change.

— Carl Rogers

- Learning without thought is labour lost. Thought without learning is intellectual death.

— Confucius

- Teaching is not a spectator sport. But is a performing art.

— D. Blocher

- Retention is best when learner is involved.

— Edward Scannell

- Thought flows in terms of stories - stories about events, stories about people, and stories about intentions and achievement. The best teachers are the best story tellers. We learn in the form of stories.

— Frank Smith
(American Psycholinguist and
Researcher of educational system
and the nature of learning)

- No man can be a good teacher unless he has feeling of warm affection toward his pupils and a genuine desire to impart to them what he believes to be of value.

— Bertrand Russell
(British philosopher, logician and mathematician)

- The task of the excellent teacher is to stimulate "apparently ordinary" people to unusual effort. The tough problem is not in identifying winners; it is in making winners out of ordinary people.

— K. Patricia Cross

- The whole art of teaching is only the art of awakening the natural curiosity of young minds for the purpose of satisfying it afterwards.

— Anatole France
(French poet, journalist and novelist)

- Teach yourself, teach everyone, his real nature, call upon the sleeping soul and see how it awakes. Power will come, glory will come, goodness will come, purity will come and everything

— Swami Vivekananda

- He who can, does.
  He who cannot, teaches,

— G.B. Shaw

- God, give us serenity to accept what cannot be changed, Courage to change what should be changed, and Wisdom to distinguish the one from the other.

— Reinhold Niebuhr

- Education makes a people easy to lead, but difficult to drive; easy to govern, but difficult to enslave.

— Lord Broughem

- A Student may easily be learning not to live, but to reason.

— Samuel Johnson

- Aristotle was asked how much educated men were superior to the uneducated.
  "As much", said he "as the living are to the dead"

— Diogenes Laertius

- I never let my schooling interfere with my education

— Mark Twain

- Failure is more often from want of energy than want of capital

Daniel Webster

- The manner of giving is worth more than the gift

— Corneille

- Knowledge is power

— Francis Bacon

- Never think that you already know all. However highly you are appraised, always have the courage to say to yourself I am ignorant

— Ivan Pavlov

- Examinations are formidable even to the best prepared, for the greatest fool can ask more than the wisest man can answer

— C. C. Colton

- I keep six honest serving-men
  (They taught me all I knew):
  Their names are What and Why and When
  And How and Where and Who

— Rudyard Kipling

- It is better to know some of the Questions than all of the Answers.

— James Thurber

- Wisdom is the power that enables us to use knowledge for the benefit of ourselves and others,

— Thomas J. Watson

- "Memory is the mother of all wisdom"

— Samuel Johnson

- "Time is more valuable than money
  You can get more money, but you cannot get more time" .

— Jim John

- Books are infinite in number and time is short and limited. The secret of knowledge is to take what is essential. Take that and try to live up to it.

— Swami Vivekananda

- Continuous effort-not strength or intelligence - is the key to unlocking our potential.

— Winston Churchill

- I was thrown out of the college for cheating on the metaphysics examination; I looked into the soul of the body sitting next to me.

— Woody Allen

- Coming together is a beginning; Keeping together is progress; Working together is success"

—Henry Ford

- "It's nice to be important, but it's more important to be nice"

— John Cassis

- "Whatever the mind can conceive and believe, the mind can achieve"

— Napoleon Hill

- Action is the foundational key to all success.

— Pablo Picasso

- "Opportunities multiply as they are seized"

— Sun Tzu

- "When books are opened, discover you have wings"

— Helen Hayes

- "Knowing is not enough; We must apply. Willing is not enough; We must do"

— Goethe

- "Integrity is who you are when no one is looking"

— John C. Maxwell

- "Never, Never, Never give up

— Sir Winston Churchill

- "The art of teaching is the art of assisting discovery"

— Mark Van Daren

- "You must be the change you wish to see in the world,

— Mahatma Gandhi

- Difficulties mastered are Opportunities won.

— Sir Winston Chruchill

- "It is not the strongest of the species that survives, nor the most intelligent that survives. It is the one that is the most adaptable to change."

— Charles Darwin

- "Better than a thousand days of diligent study is one day with a great teacher"

— Japanese Proverb

- Innovation distinguishes between a leader and a follower

— Steve Jobs

- There are no secrets to success.
  It is the result of preparation, hard work and learning from failure

— Colin Powell

- Majestic buildings and costly equipment can never be a substitute for a great, inspiring teacher.

— Dr. S. Radhakrishnan

- It is not what you **Can do**, but it is what you **Will do** which makes the difference.
- "What is caught from the teacher is more important than what is taught by the teacher"

— An old Maxim

- The meaning of communication is a response you get, and the purpose of communication is to get the desired response.
- Vision without action is a daydream. Action without vision is a nightmare

— Japanese Proverb

- Experience is the teacher of all things

— Julius Caesar

- We all have dreams. But in order to make dreams come into reality, it takes an awful lot of determination, dedication, self-discipline, and effort.

— Jesse Owens

- A product's quality is a function of how much it changes the world for the better

— Tom DeMarco

- "A teacher can never truly teach unless he is still learning himself.
  A lamp can never light another lamp unless it continues to burn its own flame."

— Rabindranath Tagore

- People don't care how much you know, till they know how much you care.
- Winners don't do different things, they do things differently.
- Management is efficiency in climbing the ladder of success;
  Leadership determines whether the ladder is leaning against the right wall.

— Stephen R. Covey

- Excellence is not a skill. It is an attitude

Ralph Morston

- Though no one can go back and make a brand new start, anyone can start from now and make a brand new end.
- Education is an ornament in prosperity and a refuge in austerity

— Aristotle

- The height you attain depends on your roots.
- Let a man learn thoroughly whatever he may learn and let his conduct be worthy of his learning

Tamil Poet: Thiruvalluvar in Kural, Chapter 40, Verse 1

- Everyone is entitled to their own opinions, but not to his own facts

— Daniel Patrick Moynihan
American Politician

- In modern society, the role of engineering is to provide systems and products that enhance the economic and social aspects of human life, thus making life easier, safer, more secure, and more enjoyable.

— Richard Fairley and Mary Willshire

- A science is as mature as its measurement tools.

— Louis Pasteur

- Working with people is difficult, but not impossible.

— Peter Drucker

- Things do not change; We change .

— Henry David Thoreau

- The secret of success is constancy to purpose

— Benjamin Disraeli

- You always pass failure on the way to success

— Mickey Rooney

- I am a slow walker, but I never walk back

— Abraham Lincoln

- The harder you work, the luckier you get.

— Gray Player

- Fortune favours the bold

— Terence

- Life shrinks or expands in proportion to one's courage

— Anais Nin

- Measure what is measurable, and what is not measurable, make it measurable

—Galileo

- Learning makes a man fit company for himself

—Thomas Fuller

- I forget what I was taught
  I only remember what I have learnt

— Patrick white

- The difference between genius and stupidity is that genius has its limits.
- Man proposes; God disposes

— Thomas a Kempis

- Laughter is the shortest distance between two people

— Victor Borge

- Knowledge is power

— Francis Bacon

- The simplest questions are the hardest to answer

— Northrop Frye

- Ideas are the building blocks of ideas

— Jason Zebehazy

- If you cannot describe what you are doing as a process,
  You don't know what you're doing

— W.E. Deming

- Life is painting a picture, not doing a sum

— Oliver Wendell Holmes

- Nothing succeeds like success

— Dumas

- To climb steep hills requires slow pace at first

— Shakespeare

- Admonish your friends privately, but praise them publicly

— Syrus

- In youth the days are short and the years are long; In old age the years are short and the days are long;

— Panin

- In simple terms, a leader is one who knows where he wants to go, and gets up, and goes

— John Er skine

- The first forty years of life gives us the text; The next thirty supply the commentary on it.

— Schopen hauer

- Well begun is half done

— Horace

- He that climbs a ladder must begin at the first round (rung)

— Scott

- A wise man does not trust all his eggs to one basket

— Cervantes

- Prosperity makes friends and adversity tries them
- Genius is one percent inspiration and ninety-nine percent perspiration

— Edison

- Time and tide wait for no man

— **Tamil Proverb**

- There is no computer that has common sense

— **Marvin Minsky**

- Success is based on imagination plus ambition and the will to work

— **Thomas Edison**

- The only place where success comes before work is in the dictionary

— **Vidal Sassoon**

- Success is a journey not a destination

— **Ben Sweetland**

- Not every group is a team, and not every team is effective

— **Glenn Parker**

- You can't always predict, but you can always prepare
- If you want to be incrementally better, Be competitive; If you want to be exponentially better; Be cooperative;
- Not everything that can be counted counts; and not everything that counts can be counted

— **Albert Einstein**

- Science is the only way to understand reality

— **Dr. Jean-Marie Lehn**
Nobel Laureate in Chemistry, 1987

- More than a discipline or a body of knowledge, engineering is a verb, an action verb, denoting a way of approaching a problem.

— **Scott Whitmire**

- A meeting is often an event in which minutes are taken and hours are wasted
- Finding good players is easy.
  Getting them to play as a team is another story

— **Casey Stengel**

- There is nothing permanent except change

— **Heraclitus, SOO BC**

- There are many ways of going forward, but only one way of standing still

— **FrankJin D. Roosevelt**

- The art of progress is to preserve order amidst change and to preserve change amidst order

— **Alfred North Whitehead**

- I would like to listen
  I have learned a great deal from listening carefully.
  Most people never listen.

— **Ernest Heminsway**

- Making mistakes is human; Repeating them is too.

— Malcolm Forbes

- Success is more a function of consistent common sense than it is of genius.

— An Wang

- It's a funny thing about life:
  If you refuse to accept anything but the best,
  You may very often get it.

— W. Somerset Maugham

- A compromise is the art of dividing a cake in such a way that everyone believes he has the biggest piece.

— Ludwig Erhard

- Quality is not an act, it is a habit

— Aristottle

- Predictions are very difficult to make, especially when they deal with the future

— Mark Twain

- The best preparation for good work tomorrow is to do good work today

— Elbert Hubbard

- Remember all things are possible for those who believe

— Gail Devers

- Dreams are pure thought, an opportunity to discover yourself.
- Life is like riding a bicycle.
  To keep your balance, you must keep moving

— Albert Einstein

- You may fool all the people some of the time; You may even fool some of the people all the time, But you can't fool all of the people all the time.

— Abraham Lincoln

- Live your life to the fullest potential, and fight for your dreams,

— Ashley Smith

- Dreams are like starts. You may never touch them, but if you follow them they will lead you to your destiny.
- Don't be pushed by your problems.
  Be led by your dreams.

23 CHAPTER GLOSSARY

College Terms you Need to Know

A

Academic Board/Committee

The higher academic body within the University system responsible for all academic standards and related policies and practices.

Academic Misconduct

Conduct in relation to any academic work that is dishonest or unfair, and includes all forms of cheating, plagiarism and lying.

Academic Record

The complete academic history of a student at the University. It includes personal details, courses completed and assessment results (marks and grades) and any awards or prizes won by the student.

Academic Staff

Faculty / Staff who have been appointed to undertake 'teaching and research' activity. Assistant Professors / Associate Professors / Professors and Deans are considered as Academic Staff/Faculty.

Academic Year

The time during the year when teaching normally takes place, generally from June/July to May (next year). The academic year consists of two semesters; Sometimes courses are offered during Summer Term also towards the end of the Academic Year.

Administration

The implementation of authorized policies and procedures and the application of systems developed within the University to achieve the agreed results and performance.

Assessment

The process by which a student's academic progress or achievement in a course/programme is evaluated. This include assignments, Quiz, submission of term-end papers, class tests, project work, seminars, tutorial participation and final examinations. Assessments in the performance and creative arts can include studio practice, modelling, creative productions, paintings, production of video and films and artistic performances and media work. Concerned faculty is responsible for evaluating the work done by student and assigning a grade of assessment to each enrolled student at the completion of the course.

Assessment needs to be aligned with the learning outcomes of the course/programme. It should be valid, reliable and consistent with the development and demonstration of skills and knowledge acquired in the professional context.

Assessment may be **formative,** providing learners with a feedback on their progress during the semester, or **summative,** providing an overall measure of achievement of a learner's performance in relation to the learning outcomes of the course as a whole at the end of the semester/year.

Assessment Grades

Student examination results in a course is normally linked with a % range of marks. Student's achievement in each course is assigned a grade of assessment. The following Letter grades are normally used.

Grade	Description	Mark (%)
D	Distinction	80 to 100%
A+	Very Good	70 to 79%
A	Good	60 to 69%
B	Pass	50 to 59%
F	Fail	Less than 50%

Assignment

An academic work submitted usually by an individual student based on the learning that occurs in class and the determination of how well the students have learnt. Although most assignments are individual, some are group assignments, submitted by a group of students on a particular topic.

Audit Agency (Quality Audit Agency)

An independent, national/international agency that conducts quality audits of universities, colleges and other higher education institutions of State and Central Universities and provides relevant Certification valid for a definite period of time (years). Such Auditing and Certification can be for a particular programme also in an University set-up.

Authentication

An IT (Information Technology) term related to checking of permission granted with a user ID and password when an authorized user logs on to a computer system.

Award (of Degree)

A recognized Certification of achievement or competency; Degree certificate is issued to a student after satisfactory completion of all the requirements of a programme/degree.

The term Award, sometimes, is also used to describe a scholarship/stipend given to support the study in a University course.

B

Bachelor's Degree

A University Degree usually requiring 3 or 4 years of fulltime or equivalent part-time study. A Bachelor's Degree qualifies a person for entry into service, occupation or a profession.

Board of Examiners

The Committee of Faculty members that examines and approves the individual student's grades and marks in the courses and determines the academic status of each student and determines the students who are to be given, Awards, Prizes and other Honours. Usually, a Dean chairs the Board of Examiners.

C

Campus

The physical location of the University/College from where a programme/course is offered. In addition to the main campus there may be campuses in other locations/countries/cities where students may be enrolled.

For online or other distance education courses, the main campus is the location where the course material/e-learning course material is developed, maintained and delivered.

Chancellor

The Chief Executive Officer/Head of the University. The Chancellor chairs the meetings of the University Council and presides over graduation ceremonies. In some Universities, the term Provost, or President is used analogus to Chancellor.

Cheating

Obtaining or attempting to obtain, or helping in obtaining, credit for academic work through any dishonest, deceptive, or fraudulent means. Cheating includes copying or using unauthorized information/sources, materials or data during a test or an examination, and the fabrication or falsification of such data.

Contact Time

The duration in a course where students are required to attend classes/periods taken by a faculty during lectures, tutorials, seminars, laboratories and workshops. Expressed in hours of instruction in a Semester.

Council (Academic Council)

The governing body that controls and manages the administration, operations, academic affairs of the University. University Academic Council consists of members of the academic staff drawn from different Departments/Schools. Meetings of the Academic Council are chaired by the Chancellor/President or by Vice-Chancellor.

Course

A programme of study necessary to qualify for an award at the University. Courses are usually identified by a course code (alpha-numeric). Some of the courses may be foundation courses, pre-requisite courses, some may be core courses/or elective courses and advanced courses.

Course Code

A sequence of usually three characters and three numbers (alpha-numeric code) used to identify each course of the University, to identify whether it is a UG or PG course, the programme, the year of study and whether foundation, core/elective or advanced course.

Course Completion

The satisfactory completion of all the academic requirements of a course including any mandatory minimum attendance, assignments, Quiz, examinations, assessments, dissertations, practicals and work experience/Project work in industry. This enables the student to become qualified for the conferring of the Award of a Degree/Diploma at graduation ceremony.

Course Coordinator

A senior Faculty responsible for the conduct and coordination of the course. The Course Coordinator is responsible to the Head of School/Department for ensuring that each course meets its learning outcomes as approved by the Academic Board, the needs of the learners, conduct of examinations and the expectations of the professional community. Also called as Programme Coordinator.

Course Learning Outcomes

The learning outcomes of the course stated clearly and in terms that enable the students to understand what skills and knowledge they are expected to achieve, and what values and attitudes will be developed by satisfactorily completing the course. The learning outcomes of the unit are usually expressed as : "On completion of this course students should be able to:" followed by the list of specific learning outcomes. The course learning outcomes are included in the curriculum outline/document.

Course Outline

A statement of the details of the course in terms of different units and how it is taught. The course outline usually contains the course title, prerequisites, credit points, learning outcomes, content, teaching method, exercises to be completed, assessment, texts and references. The course outline is a document that is approved by the School/University, providing a clear statement about the course to both the students and faculty.

Course Plan

A plan of how the course is being offered and run in a given teaching period. A course plan is a supplement to the course outline available in the curriculum document. Indicates how the course is being offered and run in the given teaching period (e.g., semester). It contains the schedule of topics/lectures, dates for Quiz, submission of assignments and end semester examinations.

Course Structure

The organization of the programme in terms of courses/subjects to be undertaken by the students in each Semester/Year, the study and evaluation scheme and the learning outcomes and other mandatory requirements for the Award of the Degree.

D

Dean

The academic head with responsibility for guiding/assisting the Faculty with strategic and policy issues and procedures and practices related to teaching and learning, research and other academic work.

Discipline (or Branch)

A field of study (or Knowledge) consisting of a related group of courses/subjects. Such fields of study/knowledge may be unitary, inter-disciplinary, cross-disciplinary, multi-disciplinary and or/ trans-disciplinary.

Distance Mode

An off-campus form of course delivery. Distance mode of delivery of a course usually refers to printed materials (study guides, work sheets, work books, assignments) being sent to individual by students mail/e-mail, and students completing the exercises and sending it back to the Faculty/ University, for evaluation and grading. Sometimes, the study materials may also be in the form of MMLP's (Multi-Media Learning Packages).

Doctoral Degree (Doctorate)

Highest University award Ph.D., D. Sc., D. Ed., or Dr. Eng. given by the University. This Degree is awarded for a substantial and original research and scholarly work which has been carried out under the guidance and supervision of a Professor/a Guide for a period of usually 3 years full-time or equivalent part-time study.

Due Date

The date (and possibly the time of the day) when an assignment is due to be submitted. The due date for each assignment is listed on the course plan/assignment sheet and date of submission of assignment written on the front page of the assignment sheet submitted by the student. Submission of an assignment after the due date may result in a lesser grade/mark.

E

Electives

Approved courses selected from the range of courses offered within the University Programme Curriculum to make up the number of credits necessary to complete a Degree. A programme may make provision for elective courses to enable students to broaden their horizons of knowledge or suit their personal interest areas/specialization.

Enabling Course/Bridge Course

A programme of study which provides bridging or supplementary education for the purpose of enabling a person to undertake programme at a University. Any deficiency in the requirements for entry can be made up by such preparation courses.

Examination

The formal, end-of-semester assessment in a course conducted during the scheduled two week examination period. Although most of the examinations are written, some are practical examinations. Students provide written answers to questions asked in the examination paper. These examinations are usually of two or three hour's duration and usually of closed books, sometimes may be open book.

In an University set-up, Controller of Examinations plans and conducts all the examinations centrally, including their supervision and evaluation of answer scripts.

External Candidate

Usually refers to a Doctoral Scholar who is working full time in an organization and has registered for a Ph.D. Programme in the University on a Part-time basis.

F

Faculty

Generally refers to a teacher/academic staff working in the College/University. Sometimes the terms may refer to an academic unit in the University e.g. Faculty of Arts, Faculty of Engineering, Faculty of Sciences, Faculty of Management, etc.

Faculty Adviser

A faculty member, working in a School/Department assigned the responsibility of advising.. and counselling students. He meets students in one-to-one or a group of students may contact the Advisor either personally or by e-mail/phone or by fax.

Foundation Courses

A set of courses. that are common to a range of programmes e.g., first year courses for which almost every student is required to register and pass.

G

General/Administrative Staff

University staff engaged in administrative and support services and who are not engaged in the academic tasks of teaching and/or research.

Graduand

A student who has completed all the requirements for the award of a Degree; waiting to get the Degree Certificate in a Graduation Ceremony/Convocation.

Graduate

A person who has received a Degree award after satisfactorily completing all the requirements of the programme. The term 'Graduate' is also used to describe a programme such as a graduate programme Mechanical Engineering.

Graduate Attributes

Generic personal attributes, skills, capacities and capabilities and values relevant for employment that help make the graduate a valuable and worthy employee. Department/School develops graduate attributes and learning outcomes/goals specific to their disciplines/programmes/ studies.

H

Head of the Department (HOD)

The senior academic with the responsibility entrusted for all the activities in the Department/ School. Each School/Department has a head for managing all the activities, related to teaching and learning within the School/Department and for carrying out R&D.

Handbook (University Hand book/Calendar)

An University publication containing essential information for all students, faculty and staff on the University facilities, procedures, rules and regulations, courses and schedule of important dates as per the Academic Calendar drawn in advance. Usually published as two Volumes, an Undergraduate Handbook and a Post-Graduate Handbook.

I

Internationalization

The process of collaborating with international institutions through an MoU (Memorandum of Understanding) for teaching, research and for carrying out joint projects for mutual benefits.

Internet

The computer communications system created for the interconnecting networks of computers around the world for exchange of information and for sending/receiving e-mails.

K

Key Performance Indicators (KPI)

A measure of key performance for an organization or a functional unit within the organization. It is an indicator of a factor critical to the success the organization.

In respect of a faculty KPI are : extent of teaching excellence, research accomplishments/ publications, and projects and Co-curricular and Extra-curricular activities carried out.

L

Learning

Improving and increasing one's knowledge of and skills in a discipline by study through instruction or by experience. Learning occurs at individual level.

Learning Approach

How and why the student learns? A learning approach has two components, a motive (why the student wants to learn) and a learning style (how the student learns). Two commonly recognized approaches to learning are the surface approach i.e. reading by glancing and the deep approach (in-depth study).

Lecture

A formal presentation by a faculty member, usually to a large number of students in a lecture class. Lectures may include the use of course material, handouts, PPT /audio-visual presentations/ aids. There are usually few opportunities for faculty-student interactions, and questioning during a lecture. However, trained faculty members encourage their students to discuss and ask questions and clarify their doubts.

M

Management for Performance

Performance of faculty and review of their academic work is carried out annually. The system provides an opportunity for faculty to discuss their performance and future goals with their supervisor/ Head of School or Department to align individual performance with organizational objectives. For new faculty, the system provides for special faculty development programmes (FDP's) and to clarify their work expectations.

% of Marks

Performance of students is indicated as a % marks obtained in a course. A range of % marks is linked to a Letter Grade.

Marking Scheme

A guideline outlining how the marks for an assessment or examination answer scripts are allocated enabling different examiners (faculty) to assess students' work fairly and consistently. The marking scheme for assessment in a subject is usually prepared by a faculty coordinator. In respect of end-semester examinations, the examiner provides a marking scheme.

Masters Degree

A university Degree designed to provide advanced theoretical and applied studies in a selected discipline. A Masters Degree usually requires an advanced study of up to two years full-time following completion of an U.G. Degree/Bachelors Degree. A Masters Degree is usually classified as a Masters Degree by Coursework and a Thesis or Masters Degree entirely by Research.

Mode of Study

A classification of the manner in which a student is undertaking a degree programme/course; Modes of study in respect of programmes are full-time, part-time (internal) or external. Sometimes the courses may be by self-study or guided study.

Modularization

A flexible course structure in which the entire course and its units are structured around a no. of independent or sequenced modules. Each individual module has a specified course content and assignments to be submitted for evaluation and grading. Some flexibility is offered in completing the modules required depending on the pace of the learner, his/her prior knowledge and interest/ individual needs.

O

Orientation Programme

A range of programmes and activities designed to assist first year students for smooth entry into University system. The University schedules orientation in the week immediately prior to the beginning of the First Semester Classes.

P

Plagiarism

The intentional or unintentional presentation as one's own work, the work of another student/ faculty/author without appropriate acknowledgement or references. The term 'work' includes all or part of any form of work including notes and papers, assignments, seminar and conference papers, reports, theses, articles, books, lecture notes and electronic submissions. Plagiarism includes;

- copying without acknowledgement of the source (or) giving references
- copying the text of another student's assignment
- copying of computer programmes, and
- copying of visual representations (line drawings, diagrams, photos)

Policies

The rules which govern student's enrolment and their academic progress in the University. Policies provide a clear statement of the University's regulations on academic and student issues and the procedures to be followed.

Postgraduate

Refers to a programme or a student; A postgraduate course is either a doctoral/master or a postgraduate diploma course. In U.S. Universities, post-graduate programmes are usually referred to as Graduate programmes. A Post-graduate student is-one who is enrolled in a postgraduate course after his under-graduate study.

Practicum

A part of a course providing learning experiences outside the University in a relevant professional setting such as an industry/organisation or Research Laboratory. During the professional placement, the student may either be an active participant or merely an observer. A practicum may cover either part of a course or many courses within the curriculum.

Prerequisite Course

A requirement that must be satisfied prior to enrolment in a specific course. A prerequisite course is usually a pass in another course (or an exemption gained from a pass in an equivalent course). Not all courses have prerequisites. All matters related to prerequisite are the responsibility of the Course/Programme Coordinator.

Programme/Degree

A field of knowledge/discipline or study comprising a related group of courses, areas of research or professional practices.

Pro Vice-Chancellor

A senior member of the faculty or a Dean with a specific responsibility assigned to help the Vice-Chancellor in academic and related issues. Pro Vice-Chancellor may also hold position as a Dean.

Q

Quality

Fitness for purpose, satisfying the requirements of objectives and specifications. Quality is related to standards meeting the specifications and the levels of attainment required.

S

School/Department

An academic unit comprising of Faculty, academic facilities and laboratories pertaining to a discipline. The School is headed by a Dean/HOD.

Semester

An academic teaching period. Normally each semester consists of 16 weeks of instruction and a final assessment/examination period (usually of two weeks). In each academic year, there are two semesters, odd semester usually between June/July and December and even semester between January and May/June.

Seminar

A seminar incorporates a lecture format combined with a discussion to follow where the presenter can answer questions or further explain the material presented. A seminar usually involves a 'small group' rather than a "large lecture group". A seminar is well suited to an audience where experts are also in the audience and they can then complement the presentation with their own experience. A seminar is usually presented in a class/lecture where the audience is in close proximity to the presenter.

Student

A learner for whom there is an enrolment in a University course at the beginning of the Semester. A student can pursue his studies on a part-time basis or on a full-time basis.

Student ID

The identification card or badge issued by the University to all students on enrolment. Each student ID may contain a code of letters and numbers allocated sequentially.

Student ID Card

The identification card issued for all students containing the student's name, his photograph, roll no. and name of the programme/course and a library bar code.

Student/Staff Ratio

The ratio between the number of full-time students taught by the Department and the number of full-time faculty in the Department.

Summer Session

A special teaching/instructional period during the summer vacation and is of a short duration usually 6 weeks; Summer session provides an opportunity to accelerate the course work, upgrade professional knowledge and/or to extend, the workplace skills and employment prospects.

T

Teacher

An academic staff member, faculty, lecturer or professor involved in the teaching of a course.

Teaching and learning Portfolio

A written, reflective document, summarizing a teacher's approach to teaching and learning, in respect of a particular course or subject and providing evidence of methods used, achievements in teaching and teaching/academic awards, and accomplishments..

Timetable

A schedule of all courses offered in a given semester showing the contact times (from ________ to____________) and room locations for all classes (lectures, tutorials, seminars, laboratories and workshops).

Tutorial

An instructional activity carried out by a faculty member, with a small number of students, structured to enable students to develop specific skills and knowledge under faculty supervision.

The tutorial provides opportunities for effective staff-student interaction, questioning and clarifying the difficult concepts taught in the lecture classes. Individual guidance is given to the students in solving difficult numerical problems.

U

Undergraduate

The term refers to a course/programme or student category. A course leading to an award of a Bachelor's Degree. An undergraduate student is one who is enrolled in an undergraduate course/programme.

V

Vice - Chancellor

The chief academic head of the University, responsible for various academic functions like teaching, R&D, Consultancy and Extension services and Community development at the University level.

W

World Wide Web

The body of software, protocols and conventions that make the internet easy for anyone to browse and use.

APPENDIX I

INDUSTRIAL TRAINING DIARY

INDUSTRIAL TRAINING PROGRAMME; GENERAL INSTRUCTIONS FOR STUDENTS

- 'Learning New Things' and 'Gaining Practical Experience' are the key objectives of industrial training programme
- Always have a Diary with you during the training period
- Follow the Training Schedule given by the industry meticulously.
- 'Be on time' everyday for training
- Carryout the assignments given by the industry daily, with all sincerity.
- Be keen to observe the new features followed in Design, Material, Production, Administration, etc., in the industry
- Make a note of such findings in the Diary, on the same day. Don't postpone
- In case of any doubt arising in the industrial processes, do not hesitate to get it clarified from the engineer/supervisor in the industry
- Do not mind soiling your hands and dress. Hands on experience will give greater confidence in you.
- Meet as many engineers as possible and engage in technical discussions with them. This will make you a confident professional
- Make friends, continue the friendship for mutual help at a future date
- Look for opportunities for taking initiatives, shouldering responsibilities, leading a team of employees on an assignment, projecting your innovative ideas for improvement etc.
- Identify the unique features of the industry in various aspects and note down in the Diary.
- "Managing Men" is the key issue for becoming a successful engineer/ manager. Learn the best practices followed in the industry and make a note of them in the Industrial Training Diary.
- Follow the rules and regulations of the industry, where you are undergoing industrial training.'

INDUSTRIAL TRAINING DIARY

Day/Week: Date: ....

Company Name: ....

Division/Section: ....

Notes: Write here what you have observed in the industry (or) what new knowledge or information you have obtained

....

....

....

....

....

....

....

....

....

....

....

....

....

....

....

....

....

....

Signature:

Date: ....

CERTIFICATE

(Issued by the Company/ Industry)

Certified that the candidate Mr. / Ms. ______________________________

Studying in ______________________________ Branch

at ______________________________ Engineering

College has undergone the prescribed industrial training in our company from ____________ to ______________ .

He/She has completed the industrial training satisfactorily as per the Training Schedule.

Signature with date

(Officer Incharge/ Industry Guide)

Company Seal

Countersigned by Industry Training Coordinator of the Department in the Engineering College

Date:

II

APPENDIX

Project Work Diary

Name of Engineering College: ....

Address : ....

Name of the Student Mr./Ms.: ....

Regn. No/Roll No. ....

Branch: ....

Project Title: ....

Name of the Guide: ....

Organization/Industry where Project Work is being carried out (with address): ....

....

....

....

....

....

....

....

....

....

....

....

....

....

Details to be Filled in only when Project Work is Carried Outside the College

1. Name of the Organization/Industry: ....
2. Address of the Organization: ....

   ....

   .... PIN ....
3. Telephone Number with STD code: ....
4. Fax: ....
5. E-Mail: ....
6. Main activity of the Organization/Industry: ....

   Products Manufactured ....
7. Name of the Industry Guide: ....
8. Name of Faculty Guide: ....
9. Designation: ....
10. Office Phone No. ....
11. Intended Period of Study: ....
12. Facilities available for students: ....

    ....
13. Timings to be followed during Project Work: ....

    ....
14. How to reach the Organization? : ....

    ....
15. Brief Description of the Intended Project: ....

    ....

    ....

    ....

    ....

Date: Signature of the Student

Signature of the External Guide Signature of the Faculty Guide

(If the Project Work is carried out in an Industry)

1. INTRODUCTION

Project Work is an important component of B.E/B.Tech Degree programme. In undergraduate level in the final semester, all students are required to carry out a Project Work either individually or in groups of two to five students.

Projects are carried out by the students under the guidance of a teaching/industry faculty. The projects could be carried out within the campus or outside the campus according to the nature of the project. If carried out outside the campus, an external/industry guide is also needed to supervise and monitor the progress of the project work.

The primary objective of a project work is to give an exposure to the students on the application of concepts and theories that they have learnt in the course. The projects can be an analysis of existing work practices or design and development of new processes, procedures and equipment or a working model or a system to solve a real life problem. The selection of project area depends on many factors including facilities available, requirements of the industry, time and interest of the students. An excellent project work can get not only good Grades but also better job offers from industries.

2. OBJECTIVES

Some specific objectives of final year students' projects are:

- To expose the students to industrial environment and work practices where manufacturing activities are carried out so that they are mentally and physically prepared to serve in an organization after their graduation
- To enable the students to observe and learn from the industry experts or practicing engineers and professionals
- To enhance the communication skills of the students by providing opportunities to discuss in groups and to present their observations, findings and report in formal reviews both in oral and written format
- To identify the relevant industry practices when compared to what are being taught in the institutional/ laboratory set-up and
- To know the latest industrial trends and improve the technical expertise of the student

Some specific problem oriented projects can also give opportunities to the students to offer new and innovative solutions in the form of suggestions or alternatives for consideration by industry/ organization for implementation.

3. PROJECT SELECTION

In the Engineering College, an introduction to project work covering need, importance, topics/ areas available for study, prospective places/ industry for doing Project Work and methodology are provided during the 6th semester. Sixth semester students attend the presentations made by eighth semester students on their project work. In the first week of eighth semester the students are grouped by the Department/Class Coordinator or on their own and then the student groups identify their study area or the project that they would like to take.

Faculty guides are assigned based on their specialization and interest. Final year Project Work Coordinator in consultation with students finalizes the student groups and guides and the same is communicated to them. (List of students in the group, Name of the Guide, Topics of project work [tentative] and Name of the company/ industry in which the project work will be carried out [if any], will be displayed in the Notice Board).

Once this process is over, the faculty guide and the team will discuss and explore the places of project work and actual title of the project work. They are expected to furnish a Preliminary Report concerning Project Work (Proforma given) to the Project Work Coordinator within two weeks from the commencement of eighth semester.

4. PROJECT SCHEDULE

Each student/team is expected to prepare a Project Schedule as per the format given. (Proforma: Project Schedule: Tentative Plan :). It will be updated as and when each activity is carried out. Effort should be made to adhere to the planned schedule. If any major deviation is noticed, then a suitable reschedule may be worked out in consultation with the Guide.

5. PROJECT SUPERVISION

1. The Project Schedule prepared by the students' shall serve as a base for guidance and supervision of the project and its progress.
2. As per the Schedule, project review meetings will be conducted periodically and recorded in the Project Work Diary
3. If a project work carried out in the college requires visits to industry/ organizations by students it should be recommended by the Guide. After visiting the industry the students should apprise the Guide about the discussion and progress made during the visit.
4. The student is expected to submit three Project Review Reports (Proforma 11: Project Review Report) to the Project Coordinator as per the Schedule. It should be signed by the student.
5. A draft version of the Report will be prepared and presented to the Guide. The observations and suggestions made shall be considered and carried out and final version of the report is submitted to the Department.
6. The Guide can explore the possibility of getting assistance to support the project from various State and National funding agencies.
7. The Guide will plan and get necessary permission and approval from the Dean/HOD for any special device required and ensure facilities needed for the completion of the project is available
8. It will be the responsibility of the Guide to ensure that the project is useful to the student and the industry. Students can be encouraged to develop a new system, new model, carry out a small scale research and publication of a paper. Faculty Guide should ensure that the project work could be completed well within the time frame available.
9. If a project work is carried out by a group of students, the tasks assigned and carried out by individual members towards the progress of the project will also be recorded in the Proforma 18.
10. At the end of the project, student is expected to give individual feedback about the project work and the benefits derived (Proforma 19)

6. OUTCOME OF THE PROJECT

One or more of the following are generally expected as outcome of the Project Work:

- Innovative solution to the selected problem
- Development of new design/circuit/product/process/layout/procedure/model
- Critical analysis of existing practices and offering suggestions for improvements
- New Software Development/Development of a new Algorithm
- Publication of a Paper in a technical journal/ presentation of a paper in a conference
- Application and Registration of a Patent

7. PROJECT EVALUATION & SCHEME OF ASSESSMENT

Suggested criteria for assessment of the project work are:

Continuous/Semester Assessment			Final Examination	
	Criteria	Maximum Marks	Criteria	Maximum Marks
1	Literature Survey and Problem Definition	20	Presentation & Viva voce'	50
2	Methodology & Plan of work (I Review	20	Project Report	50
3	Word carried out (II Reveiw)	20		
4	Results and Analysis (III Review)	20		
5	Final Report	20		
	Total	100	Total	100

8. PRELIMINARY REPORT CONCERNING THE PROJECT WORK

Name of the Student Mr./Ms.: ....

Registration No/Roll No: ....

Branch: ....

Faculty Guide's Name: ....

or/and Industry Guide's Name: ....

Broad area of Study: ....

....

Place where Project work will be carried out ....

....

Specific Problem Identified/Proposed Project Title: ....

....

....

Date: Signature of the Student

Signature of the Industry Guide Signature of the Faculty Guide

(If the Project Work is carried out in an Industry)

9. PROJECT SCHEDULE [TENTATIVE PLAN]

Name of the Student Mr./Ms.: ....

Branch of Study: ....

Faculty Guide's Name: ....

Project Title: ....

[Identify main activities in your project work and write down here in a chronological order with its target date]

Major Activities	Target Date
Preliminary Report concerning the Project Work	
Finalization of Objectives and Methodology	
Review – I	
Review – II	
Review – III	
Submission of draft version of Final Report	
Presentation & Viva-Voce	

Date:

Signature of the Student

Signature of the Guide

10. RECORD OF ACTIVITIES CARRIED OUT BY THE STUDENT IN MONTH - 1

Month: .... **Year..............................**

[You may also record here the points discussed]

WEEK	ACTIVITIES CARRIED OUT DURING THE WEEK
1st Week	
2nd Week	
3rd Week	
4th Week	

Signature of Faculty/Industry Guide:

Name of the Guide:

Date:

11. PROJECT REVIEW REPORT - 1

Name of the Student: ....

Register No. / Roll No.: ....

Branch of Study: ....

Faculty Guide's Name/Industry Guide's Name:

....

Project Title: ....

Status of the Project: ....

....

Date: Signature of the Student

Remarks by Guide: ....

Signature of the Guide with Date

Project Review Report should be submitted during reviews'. This report shall give the details of work carried out till now and progress of the project work.

12. RECORD OF ACTIVITIES CARRIED OUT BY THE STUDENT IN MONTH 2

Month: .... **Year..............................**

[You may also record here the points discussed]

WEEK	ACTIVITIES CARRIED OUT DURING THE WEEK
1st Week	
2nd Week	
3rd Week	
4th Week	

Signature of Faculty/Industry Guide:

Name of the Guide:

Date:

13. PROJECT REVIEW REPORT - 2

Name of the Student: ....

Register No. / Roll No.: ....

Branch of Study: ....

Faculty Guide's Name/Industry Guide's Name:

....

Project Title: ....

Status of the Project: ....

....

Date: Signature of the Student

Remarks by Guide: ....

Signature of the Guide with Date

Project Review Report should be submitted during reviews. This report shall give the details of work carried out till now and progress of the project work.

14. RECORD OF ACTIVITIES CARRIED OUT BY THE STUDENT IN MONTH - 3

Month: .... **Year...............................**

[You may also record here the points discussed]

WEEK	ACTIVITIES CARRIED OUT DURING THE WEEK
1st Week	
2nd Week	
3rd Week	
4th Week	

Signature of Faculty/Industry Guide:

Name of the Guide:

Date:

15. PROJECT REVIEW REPORT - 3

Name of the Student: ....

Register No. / Roll No.: ....

Branch of Study: ....

Faculty Guide's Name/Industry Guide's Name:

....

Project Title: ....

....

Status of the Project: ....

....

Date: Signature of the Student

Remarks by Guide: ....

Signature of the Guide with Date

Project Review Report should be submitted during reviews. This report shall give the details of work carried out till now and progress of the project work.

16. A RECORD OF INTERACTION/ DISCUSSIONS BETWEEN STUDENT AND FACULTY/ INDUSTRY GUIDE DURING THE PROJECT WORK

Date	Points Discussed/Action Proposed

Signature of Faculty/ Industry Guide:

Name of the Guide:

Date:

17. Record of Challenges Faced by Student(s) During the Project Work and How was It Solved

Project Title: ....

....

[Record here major hurdles/ problems faced by you/ your team in completing the project work. Briefly discuss what steps have been taken to overcome or to solve the problems, if any]

S.No.	Major Problems/Challenges	How was it solved?

18. Project Work Undertaken by a Group of Students

If a project work is carried out by a group of students, list out the tasks assigned and carried out by each member. This information is required to know the specific contribution made by each member of the group in carrying out the project work.

Name of the Members in the Group	Tasks Assigned/Major Work Carried Out
Your Name	
Names of the other Members in the group	
Name (1)	
Name (2)	
Name (3)	

Guide's Remarks:

Signature of Guide

Date:

19. Student's Feedback

Name of the Student Mr./Ms.: ....

Registration No/Roll No: ....

Branch of Study: ....

Faculty/Industry Guide's Name: ....

....

Project Title: ....

....

....

Name of the Organization: ....

Write your feedback in respect of Project work you have carried out/benefits you have derived.

....

....

....

....